HEALING
MANDALAS

HEALING MANDALAS

30 INSPIRING MEDITATIONS TO SOOTHE YOUR MIND, BODY & SOUL

LISA TENZIN-DOLMA

DUNCAN BAIRD PUBLISHERS
LONDON

Healing Mandalas
Lisa Tenzin-Dolma

Distributed in the USA and Canada by
Sterling Publishing Co., Inc.
387 Park Avenue South
New York, NY 10016-8810

This edition first published in the UK and USA in 2008 by
Duncan Baird Publishers Ltd
Sixth Floor, Castle House
75–76 Wells Street
London W1T 3QH

Managing Editor: Kelly Thompson
Editor: Susannah Marriott
Editorial Assistants: Emma Maule, Kirty Topiwala
Managing Designer: Dan Sturges
Designer: Sue Bush
Picture Researcher: Julia Ruxton
Commissioned artwork: Rowena Dugdale

Library of Congress Cataloging-in-Publication Data available

ISBN-13: 978-1-84483-616-1   ISBN-10: 1-84483-616-9

1 3 5 7 9 10 8 6 4 2

Typeset in Adobe Jenson Pro and ITC Franklin Gothic
Color reproduction by Colourscan
Printed in China

For information about custom editions, special sales, premium and corporate purchases, please contact
Sterling Special Sales Department at 800-805-5489 or specialsales@sterlingpub.com.

Notes:
Abbreviations used throughout this book:
CE Common Era (the equivalent of AD)
BCE Before the Common Era (the equivalent of BC)
b. born, d. died

I saw that everything, all paths I had been following, all steps I had taken, were leading back to a single point—namely, to the mid-point. It became increasingly plain to me that the mandala is the center. It is the exponent of all paths. It is the path to the center, to individuation ... I knew that in finding the mandala as an expression of the self I had attained what was for me the ultimate.

C. G. JUNG (1875–1961)

CONTENTS

INTRODUCTION:
A PATH TO
WHOLENESS

FINDING THE
WHOLE SELF

54 **Spiral of Life**
Nurturing potential

56 **Self in the Cosmos**
Finding our place

60 **Eternal Om**
Enhancing self-expression

64 **Moonlight Epiphany**
Trusting intuition

68 **The Unfolding Now**
Living in the present moment

70 **Healing Motion**
Embracing change

74 **Jewel in the Lotus**
Honouring inner beauty

78 **Rippling Waters**
Cultivating a still mind

80 **Wild-Horse Winds**
Breaking shackles

84 **Triple Spiral**
Integrating mind,
body and spirit

THE SELF
AND OTHERS

88 **Rainbow Union**
Balancing opposites

92 **Healing Mirror**
Closing the hands
in prayer

94 **Two Trees, One Root**
Blossoming together

96 **A Dome over All**
Seeking the divine

100 **Wings of Peace**
Healing a quarrel

104 **Mystic Rings**
Connecting through love

106 **Like a Butterfly**
Fostering freedom

110 **Lady of Compassion**
Offering loving-kindness

114 **A Cup Overflowing**
Bestowing forgiveness

118 **Another's Fire**
Projecting beyond the self

THE SELF IN TIMES OF CHALLENGE

124 Spiral River
Going with the flow

128 Floating Clouds
Letting go of fear

130 Teardrop Healing
Dealing with grief

134 Regenerating Sun
Rediscovering energy

136 The All-Seeing Eye
Accessing your wise self

140 Phoenix Rising
Recovering your health

144 Dragon Power
Calling on your
protective powers

148 Golden Cross
Sourcing inner strength

152 The Jaws of the Lion
Fortifying the soul

154 Lotus Harvest
Gathering in peace

158 Further reading
159 General index
160 Index to symbols
161 Acknowledgments

A PATH TO WHOLENESS

AS WE REST OUR GAZE UPON A MANDALA, THE MIND BECOMES AS STILL
AS THE SURFACE OF A POOL OF WATER. FROM THE PROFOUND DEPTHS
OF TRANQUILLITY EMERGE INSIGHTS THAT HELP US TO TAP INTO
AND DEVELOP OUR INNATE HEALING POWERS.

A mandala is a symbolic picture or pattern used in meditation. Its various motifs, its colours and its geometry are specifically designed to bring about inner focus and inner peace. Mandalas most often take the form of a circle – a shape that represents the self, the Earth, the Sun, the cosmos and the state of wholeness that is the ultimate aim of mandala meditation. By taking this path we move toward a state of completeness and a realization of our true nature, which, like the circle of the mandala, is boundless and perfect. Experiencing such a deep sense of unity is immensely healing.

The unique pressures of modern living make the need for healing more prevalent now than ever. As we work longer hours, commute further and often don't take enough time to eat healthily, exercise or unwind, so the statistics for

Left: Droplets of rain falling on the calm surface of still water cause gentle ripples to flow outward in perfect circles: one of the natural symbols that reflect the harmony of the cosmos.

stress-related illness rise. The high expectations that we set ourselves strain our physical, mental and emotional resources, and may lead to physical symptoms, relationship problems or a generalized sense of lack of fulfilment. All are messages we should take notice of and act upon.

Fortunately, body and mind have an immense capacity for self-regeneration. And if we slow down and dive within, we can create space for this to develop. Try this experiment. Clench your fist and see what happens. You probably feel tense and closed-in. Then relax your hand. Do you feel more open, more receptive? The same principle applies to the mind: when it is stressed and cluttered, your body will feel tense, but when your mind is quiet, the body follows suit, relaxing in a way that allows our innate healing processes to begin their work.

Healing begins at a profound level that we cannot control consciously. It might feel spontaneous and immediate, like a cog slipping into place. Or it might evolve over time. Mandala meditation allows you to encourage healing at a pace that is right for you. By setting aside a little time every day to look at a mandala – ten minutes makes a good start – you will take the first steps on a journey away from anxiety and stress toward the increased balance, optimism and freedom that come from reconnecting with your inner resources and gaining a fresh perspective on life's challenges.

ENERGY HEALING

To restore equilibrium to our often unbalanced lifestyles, many of us turn to complementary therapies such as homeopathy, acupuncture, reiki and colour therapy. Although these therapies adopt different methods, they all take as their starting point the principle that there are energies at work within the body. Imbalances within our energy system, if left untreated, can manifest as symptoms of illness. But harmony can be restored by therapies using subtle adjustments whose workings cannot be explained by Western science.

In homeopathy, "new vibrations" are introduced to our energy systems in the form of pills or tinctures that include minute amounts of a substance shaken at high speed to increase its vibrational force. In acupuncture treatments, fine needles are inserted into energy points on the body to undo blockages in our "meridians" — the channels through which energy circulates. In reiki, a healer channels energy through his or her hands.

It is beyond the scope of this book to argue that mandala meditation can heal in similar ways by bringing harmony to our energy systems — although such a view would have its adherents. The subject, of course, is controversial: orthodox medicine is increasingly working in alliance with complementary therapies but there are plenty of nay-sayers still.

The case in favour of mandala meditation can be made modestly, without migrating to the outer fringes of the mind-body-spirit movement. The influence of the mind on the state of the body is well established: think of placebos, of the physical symptoms of stress, of the way in which we can train ourselves to overcome phobias and anxieties, and of the proven power of hypnosis. Buddhists sometimes use the analogy of rust, which comes from iron, yet can destroy iron. In the same way, a negative state of mind can hasten the destructive power of illness; while conversely, positive feelings may provide a bulwark against many ailments. Meditation can release tension and prime the mind to allow the body's immunity defences to work at full strength. No one loses anything by trying.

THE POWER OF MEDITATION

There are many forms of meditation. You can observe or count your breath (in, out, in, out) or gaze at a candle until you feel a sense of unity with the flame. In mantra meditation you repeat a word or phrase designed to positively influence both your mind and body. And in mandala meditation you let your gaze settle on a circular image. In all forms, the ultimate aim is to dissolve differences between you and the object of meditation: to close the gap that makes you feel separate.

Any form of meditation has enormous benefits for physical, mental *and* emotional health. The psychological effects of meditation include a reduction in anxiety, moodiness and depression, improved memory and self-esteem, and increased emotional stability and happiness. Physically, meditation has been shown in numerous studies to lower blood pressure, enhance the immune system and relax the body, leading to a healthier heart-rate. On a more spiritual level, meditation enhances your perception and intuition, and helps to open up a deep well of inner wisdom and compassion, and a sense of higher connection.

Meditation is recommended by more and more doctors as a tool to enhance and speed up the healing process, especially for certain medical conditions, such as high blood pressure. The method combines well with conventional treatment and has no adverse side effects or contraindications.

MANDALA MEDITATION FOR EVERYONE

Mandalas are particularly broad-ranging meditation tools. They can be used by beginners and experienced practitioners of meditation alike, and there is no need to undergo a period of tutoring or self-discipline. Many other forms of meditation require regular practice to train the mind, but anyone can simply sit with a mandala and soon begin to gain benefits.

Mandalas are designed so that your eye and attention are naturally drawn to certain areas in the structure and then progressively led through other imagery – it can feel like taking a relaxed walk on a sunny day. You can benefit from spending just ten minutes with a mandala, but if you allow this to extend to fifteen or twenty minutes at a sitting, you will experience the positive effects more profoundly. Soon you will notice that you feel more relaxed, your concentration is sharper, and your thoughts and responses more effective. In this state of underlying calm, any irritation or disappointment that comes along is less likely to seem important, and it will therefore become easier to maintain equanimity.

It can be useful to keep a journal after mandala meditation. Note any thoughts and issues, reflections and insights that come to light. Sometimes the healing process involves recognizing patterns that you might previously have denied – simple recognition can allow you to start making changes.

A FIRST MANDALA MEDITATION

In this meditation, a photograph of the Earth as seen from space, opposite, serves as a mandala. Sit comfortably on a cushion or chair in a place where you won't be disturbed, and place the page at eye level, about arm's length away.

1   Take three very deep, slow breaths, and then return to normal, steady and even breathing throughout the exercise.

2   Rest your gaze on the image, keeping your eyes softly focused. Try not to stare at it, nor to let your mind wander to random thoughts about the continents or countries. Simply allow the image and its patternings to soak into your consciousness. Keep coming back to this.

3   Ultimately, let there be no distinction between you and the globe. View it as outside of you, yet sitting in the depths of your mind. You are also a tiny form on the planet's surface – relax into this feeling of connectedness.

4   After five or ten minutes, or when you feel ready to stop, take three deep, slow breaths, then breathe normally again. Close your eyes for a moment, stretch and wriggle your fingers and toes. Take a few minutes to bathe in the feelings of relaxation and peace. Consider any ideas or insights that occur to you, and, if you wish, write them down in a journal.

MORE THAN MEDITATION

Healing is synonymous with "becoming whole" – attaining a state of internal and external harmony. To heal, we must bring imbalances in the mind and heart back into a state of equilibrium, which in turn has a positive effect on the body. However, mandala meditation is about more than this: it also makes us more whole by strengthening our connection with our essential nature.

The psychologist Carl Jung (1875–1961) asserted that mandalas are a key to personal transformation because they represent "an archetype of wholeness". Through the power of their symbolism, they allow us to apprehend the manifold aspects of the cosmos (the macrocosm) reflected in each of us (the microcosm), albeit unknowingly. Contemplating a mandala expands our limited perspective to show us the interconnectedness of everything in the universe. This makes us feel more complete and gives an insight into our spiritual nature. We free ourselves from unhelpful ways of thinking that prevent our inner growth. If we consciously use this new way of seeing to cultivate inner harmony during testing times, we begin to react more constructively to everyday stresses. This healing benefits all areas of life – from relationships with our partner, friends and family to our career and our creative projects – and filters through to create well-being in the body as well as in the mind and heart.

MANDALAS IN DIFFERENT TRADITIONS

Humankind has created mandala-like designs since earliest times, across different cultures and faith traditions, with whatever materials have been to hand. Our distant ancestors left marks on the walls of caves, traced patterns in sand and placed stones in sacred alignments, such as those at Stonehenge in England and Carnac in France. More readily associated with meditation are the Eastern designs that are now familiar in the West. But creating mandalas is a *living* tradition, whether the images are pixellated on a computer or hand-wrought onto paper, silk, canvas or sand.

Mandalas have always been viewed as a path to enlightenment – a method by which our mind can connect with the life-force of the universe and so attain liberation. In Indian, Tibetan and Chinese versions they traditionally depict cultural symbols, sometimes including deities, to express in pictorial form the profound nature of reality. The Tibetan Kalachakra deity, to take just one example, lies at the centre of a mandala that is considered his sacred palace and is used in tantric spiritual initiation rites as well as for healing. The centre where he sits is the matrix: the "all" from which everything manifests. After the rites, the complex mandala, executed in coloured sands made up of precious stones finely crushed, is swept away as a lesson in impermanence.

Large-scale "mandalas" formed by alignments of stones in the landscape may possibly have a global purpose beyond the spiritual healing of the community. Like giant acupuncture needles, they may seek to optimize the energy of the planet, as they tend to be sited on powerful earth-energy points along meridians crisscrossing the land. They also connect with the universe as astronomic observatories, their alignments charting the movements of heavenly bodies. The Native American medicine wheel, a circle of rocks with radiating spokes made from smaller stones, also tracks astronomical alignments. Indigenous Australian sand mandalas invoke a time of creation, known as the Dreamtime, when the laws of the universe came into being, as well as strengthening the people's connections with the land.

The Indian science of Vastu uses a giant mandala to bring new buildings and even town-planning in line with terrestrial and cosmic forces, thereby harnessing positive energy and healing. The Dogon people in Mali, Africa, construct their homes in the shape of a mandala that echoes the cosmos: the dwellings are built in pairs to represent Heaven and Earth, while the ground is dug in spirals to follow the energy of the earth. Much smaller domestic mandalas, such as Native American dreamcatchers and medicine shields and Chinese feng-shui diagrams, bring potent healing energy and protection right into the heart of the home.

Left: A Native American medicine wheel in Arizona. The circular forms and internal structures of medicine wheels reflect complex astrological alignments and, just like mandalas, can be used as tools for meditation.

MAPS OF WELL-BEING

A mandala can be thought of as a map that leads us to a tranquil inner state – to what Carl Jung called "a safe refuge of inner reconciliation and wholeness". Along the way we glimpse different aspects of our multi-faceted psyche, which we may not have been aware of previously. As with any route-map, the mandala has a starting-point from which we take our first step on the journey toward wholeness. Liberated from the everyday constraints of space and time, we embark from here on our inner adventure. Traditionally, the initial point of focus is a dot at the centre of the circle, from which the eye travels outward; however, with some mandalas we may start at the outer rim, from which we move inward. A mandala's central focal point is known as the *bindu*, a Sanskrit word meaning "drop". It is helpful to imagine this as a safe place of stillness, where you can rediscover your true self and open up to the possibilities contained in the mandala. Once you connect with the energy of this point, you can experience it anywhere in the mandala.

From the *bindu*, the mandala map opens out like the petals of a rose to reveal multiple layers of reality. Each motif represents a different aspect of your psyche as well as some aspect within the cosmos. Resting your gaze on the motifs one by one, or all together in a single overview, leads you on a twofold voyage inward to the heart of the self and outward to explore the cosmos. Once you are in a relaxed state of mind, moving your eyes slowly over the symbols of the mandala relaxes you further. It also stimulates a blossoming that begins deep within and spreads all through your being. You are well placed now to allow the opposites within yourself to be harmonized and the healing energies of the design to exert their benign influence. Slowing down and penetrating deeper into wordless understanding, you discover the real you.

MANDALAS AND THE MIND

The symmetries, repetitions and contrasts of mandala patterns create a hypnotic effect that can cause changes in the rhythms of your brainwaves. This is nothing to be worried about: you experience this simply as a subtle shift in perspective and a sensation of greater serenity. As in all forms of meditation, contemplating a mandala settles the mind into first an Alpha and then a Theta state (see right), which has proven benefits for mind and body, from a reduction in heart and pulse rates and easier breathing to strengthened immunity.

Beta brainwave rhythm (30–40 HZ) Corresponds with a state of alertness and concentration.

Alpha brainwave rhythm (7–12 HZ) Associated with a state of relaxation. In this state, your ability to visualize and to be creative is stimulated.

Theta brainwave rhythm (4–7 HZ) At the fringes of consciousness, this state of being nourishes intuition and memory. It also encourages insight and deep healing.

Delta brainwave rhythm (0–4 HZ) Correlates with a state of deep sleep.

SYMBOLS OF THE UNCONSCIOUS

Jungian psychology identifies several layers of consciousness. As well as the individual's waking conscious (thoughts, memories and perceptions) and personal unconscious (dreams and forgotten memories), and what might be called the "collective consciousness" (the beliefs, perceptions and experiences common to everyone), there is the collective unconscious (a shared, cross-cultural collection of archetypes, or universal images, that carry underlying symbolic meaning). The archetypes are thought to be present in the "self", but most of us are only

KEY ELEMENTS OF A MANDALA

The most important elements of a mandala's form are designed to work together to bring about a change in consciousness and, ultimately, a harmony of mind and body.

Bindu The central "seed" of the mandala is an intense concentration of energy, and a starting point for your inner exploration. It may be seen as the bottomless well of the self.

Circle Symbolizes the whole, and spiritual perfection. It can also represent the state of completeness that meditation fosters.

Square Shows the physical world and directions: north, south, east and west. Ground yourself here as you bring about inner transformation.

Perimeter The energy of the mandala is contained by this outer rim, which also allows your mind to work within familiar boundaries.

Right: Traditional Tibetan mandalas are complex compositions, rich in symbolism, representing the palace of the gods. Mandalas have been used for meditation and healing in Asia for over a thousand years.

ever aware of a few of them – they may surface in dreams or in creative work in various media. Of interest to practitioners of meditation are those archetypes – for example, certain deities and animals – that appear in mandalas.

Our drive as human beings, according to Jungian thought, is to experience a state of "individuation" – of becoming whole within ourselves. Meditating on a mandala helps us toward individuation because it allows us to explore and apprehend many aspects of the self – all those elements (including the archetypes of the collective unconscious) that we don't even know we have within us – and to bring them into focus. Let us take just two examples. Jung identifies the Anima, which is the feminine image within a male psyche, and the Animus, which is the masculine image in a female psyche. Meditating on the Anima or Animus within a mandala can help to attune you to the complementary gender within yourself, and all its qualities of compassion and intuition (Anima) and action and decisiveness (Animus).

The insights that follow mandala meditation are unique to you, the meditator: they reflect the discoveries you will have made in the course of a rewarding inward adventure.

It can be helpful to think about the images within a mandala as we think about the motifs in dreams. When we dream, we journey not only into our personal unconscious, but also into the collective unconscious, which is why dream symbols sometimes seem to express a universal language. In dreams, as in meditation, we are in the realm of intuition, not reason. We respond to images in ways that by-pass our faculties of reason. We may later intellectualize the experience, but what matters is our direct response to the power of symbols – one that takes place at subconscious levels of the self. It is at these innermost levels of being that the healing energies of mandalas are effective.

The motifs within the mandalas in this book have been specially chosen to encourage different kinds of healing through our intuitive response to symbolism. Each mandala has been carefully designed to achieve particular effects – for example, to ease anxiety, to calm the mind, to foster self-belief, to mend or strengthen relationships, and to help us to cope in times of challenge.

THE POWER OF FOCUS

When iron filings are scattered onto a sheet of paper, they fall randomly, perhaps in clusters of various sizes. Then, if you place a magnet beneath the sheet, you will see the filings re-organize themselves in a pattern around the magnet's poles. This is the power of magnetic attraction, and it is a helpful model for understanding some of the powers of the mind.

Thoughts tend to pass in a wayward manner through our minds, according to our moods, our most deep-rooted preoccupations and the various external stimuli to which we are subjected. Generally, our thoughts are active and unruly unless consciously brought to a focus – as they are, for example, when you concentrate on a task. When you do so, the filings cluster around the poles of your intention and around the steps you take mentally to carry out that intention. Instead of chaos there is order.

It is interesting to see what happens when we make a space for our thoughts, and then within this space refuse to dwell on the negative. Inevitably, anxieties or other negative thoughts will invade our space, in their usual random way, but we have the option to just let them drift away, out of our minds. They can only stay if we allow them to. Positive thoughts, on the other hand, may be encouraged: if we give them our permission, we will benefit from their influence. Now, this "space", as we have called it, could simply be the backdrop of consciousness, the mind itself. But it could also be the mandala on which you meditate.

In a mandala, we generate an arena that allows only positive thoughts into its circle. It isn't that we are concentrating hard upon a task: the process is more open than that. It's more that we have created a filter, so that only positive thoughts are allowed to linger, while negative ones are ignored. You will have

HEALING ENERGY PRACTICE

This exercise uses the image of the globe on page 15 as a mandala once again. However, this time as you gaze at the image, you extend your meditation beyond the mandala until you can imagine yourself absorbing healing energy from the universe itself. After charging your reserves of healing energy, you practise directing it in a positive way. Start by sitting comfortably on the floor or on a chair in a place where you won't be disturbed. Prop up the globe image at arm's length in front of you.

1 Let your gaze settle on the image of the globe for two or three minutes. Keep your eyes soft, rather than staring, and do not analyze the picture. Instead, simply allow its patternings to rest in your consciousness.

2 Now take your focus inside yourself, imagining yourself as the globe. Feel powerful, beautiful and complete. Remind yourself that you are innately whole and perfectly balanced. Retaining this reassuring idea, contemplate your unique purpose and the contribution you can make.

3 After a few minutes, let your attention drift. Feel as though you are floating through space. Then begin to look afresh at the image of the globe in front of you. Appreciate its unique form from a distance, observing its luminous beauty as it hangs in space. Now tell yourself that you are larger than the Earth. Feel a part of the entire cosmos. Bathe in this sensation, breathing evenly, for a few minutes.

4 Because you are now part of the cosmos, tell yourself that you have access to its infinite resources. With each breath, draw in healing energy from the universe. After a while, direct this energy to wherever you feel it is needed in your body and your life.

5 When you are ready to stop, take three deep breaths, exhaling fully. Then breathe normally again. Close your eyes and sit quietly for at least five more minutes. Then open your eyes, wriggle your fingers and toes, have a stretch and look around. Note any feelings, thoughts or insights in a journal, if you wish.

gathered by now that the positive thoughts arise, in the first place, from the energies of the mandala's symbolism. We open ourselves to the influence of the mandala, and allow our minds to focus lightly on its forms and symbols.

MANDALAS AND MEDITATION

At this point it might be helpful to recap on what a mandala is and say a little more about how the device is used in meditation. Essentially, a mandala is a sacred image which, when we focus on it, draws our attention inward and enables us to intuitively apprehend its symbolic meaning and absorb this into our mind. Meditating on a mandala takes us on a journey into our wise centre which is in harmony with the cosmos. This involves mental and physical relaxation without any loss of alertness.

To begin with you might be interested in focusing on separate aspects of the mandala, engaging with their symbolism and ticking off the associations you can recognize – for example, the lotus as purity, the dove as hope and faith, the phoenix as rebirth. The healing mandalas in this book are accompanied by a kind of "pre-meditation" tour of their symbolism, to acquaint you with some of the thinking that has influenced the visual details. However, when meditating in the true sense of the word, it is important that you cast aside, at the conscious level, what you have learned about the symbolic content of the imagery. The aim of this more mature kind of meditation is to just let the mandala make an impression on you without trying to analyze it. You put your powers of logical reasoning on hold and rely instead on intuition. Naturally, you will have been influenced by what you have read of the symbols, by what you already knew of them, and by the subconscious associations that all of us experience when exposed to archetypes. Such preconditioning enriches the meditative experience. But during the time of meditation itself, you do not consciously draw upon this knowledge: instead you relax into your intuition.

Do not worry, if at any point during your meditations with mandalas, you are unsure whether to look at the symbols individually or at the design as a whole: this is unimportant. For some of the time, however, it is helpful to let the *entire* image rest in your mind. Obviously, when you try this, you cannot focus on *all* the details within the mandala's perimeter; some degree of "defocusing" will be necessary. Do not be concerned if your eyes are drawn to details: just "defocus" again when you notice this is happening, and return to the image as a whole. A good way to do this is to start with the mandala's overall geometry. Above all, just let things happen, in a state of relaxed attention. There are no rules that require you to think particular thoughts.

HEALING WITH SUBTLE ENERGY

In order to understand a little more about how mandalas can bring about positive change, it is useful to learn about the force-field of subtle energy, known as an aura, which is thought to surround all living things. Some healers literally see this intangible "body" of energy as interpenetrating layers of subtly glowing colours, which follow the body's contours and reveal information about your health, emotions and spiritual development: the fine web of the aura is said to

CHAKRA ASSOCIATIONS

Each chakra, or subtle energy centre, is linked to a part of the body and presides over a range of emotional, intellectual and spiritual responses.

Root chakra Located around the base of the spine, at the perineum, this chakra is associated with survival, security and instinct.

Sacral chakra Found just above the pubic bones, this chakra presides over sexuality and creativity.

Solar-plexus chakra Felt just above the navel, this chakra governs energy, drive and motivation.

Heart chakra At the centre of the chest, level with the heart, this chakra relates to loving emotions.

Throat chakra Sensed around the hollow at the base of the throat, this chakra is linked to communication and healthy self-expression.

Third-eye chakra Found at the centre of the forehead, this is the mind's eye, where you relate to your intuition and visionary capacity.

Crown chakra Felt at the crown of the head, this is the highest chakra, which presides over consciousness and spiritual insight.

become distorted or torn around areas of disease, and the colours are thought to vary in luminosity according to your emotional state. The deep breathing that mandala meditation promotes is thought to strengthen the aura, making its colours appear more vibrant – a sign of good health.

Within the energy of the aura lie the seven major chakras (see box, opposite), centres of subtle energy visualized as wheels that gather life-force and distribute it to the various realms of the body, emotions and intellect. Each chakra governs a particular set of physical, mental and emotional processes, which becomes more refined as we move up the chakra system: for example, our instinct for security and survival is ruled by the root, or base, chakra, situated around the perineum, while spiritual insight is determined at the highest chakra, sited at the crown of the head.

Because the colours, shapes and many of the archetypal images found in mandalas are linked with particular chakras, you may find yourself drawn to a mandala because you have a specific, often unconscious, need for healing in the realm of the body ruled by that chakra. As your gaze rests upon the mandala, the chakra is stimulated to rebalance the flow of energy to its corresponding parts of the body, emotions or intellect, improving your health and the way in which you can respond to problems caused by the world and people around you.

THE POWER OF COLOUR

Colours have an impact on our emotions and moods. It is hard to sustain the case that these associations are necessarily universal, as some of them are culturally determined: for example, in certain countries the hue of mourning is not black but white. Even so, there are numerous equivalences that can be taken as standard. By opting for a certain colour, in our dress or in our environment, we can go some way toward lifting a bad mood or increasing our energy levels. Research has shown that colour choice may even be able to boost immunity or speed the recovery of hospital patients following an operation.

One of the first things that may draw us to a particular mandala is its palette of colours. By focusing on particular colours within the design during your meditation, you can open yourself to their beneficial energies. What is at work here are the different wavelengths of light, which manifest as various colours. The waves become shorter as the seven colours of the rainbow move in a continuous spectrum from red at one end through orange, yellow, green, blue, and indigo to violet at the other end. Each vibration is said by energy healers to affect your aura by balancing the chakra with which that colour is associated (see box, opposite). You might find yourself drawn to colours in a mandala that relate to areas of the body or psyche that require healing most urgently.

COLOUR SYMBOLISM

The following colours have a particular energy profile and chakra association, alongside their traditional symbolism.

Red The colour of blood, red is energizing and warming. It can increase vitality, joy, passion and motivation. Connected with the root chakra, red stimulates the survival instinct, counters low energy and strengthens the organs of elimination. Too much can cause aggression.

Orange Traditionally the hue of fertility, love and splendour, orange brings upbeat, happy emotions. It is linked with the sacral chakra and used to stimulate creativity, positivity and sexual energy.

Yellow Although linked with treachery in China and elsewhere, this colour generally fosters cheerfulness and strengthens memory and intellect. It can also help to increase commitment. Yellow links with the solar-plexus chakra and is used to boost the digestive system, pancreas and adrenal glands.

Green Associated with growth, spring, youth and renewal, green has calming, harmonizing qualities, and can help to relieve anxiety and stress. It links with the heart chakra and is used to balance the immune system, lungs and heart. Green helps us to deal with issues of love, self-esteem and relationships with others.

Blue Cooling and soothing, blue encourages a sense of tranquillity. It is also symbolic of infinity, devotion, faith and chastity. Linked with the throat chakra, blue is used to ease throat ailments and unblock problems with communication.

Indigo A spiritually uplifting hue, indigo helps to calm the mind and promote restful sleep. This colour is associated with the third-eye chakra, stimulates the pineal gland and promotes inspiration.

Violet This colour fosters spiritual refinement and insight. Linked with the crown chakra, it stimulates the pituitary gland, hormones and growth.

SYMBOLS OF HEALING

Images are more ancient and universal than alphabets, words or writing, for they tap into our collective unconscious (see page 24). Throughout history and all across the world they have been used to express feelings, provoke reactions, tell stories and embody philosophies – as well as to heal and increase a sense of connection with nature and with our spiritual source.

Although the meanings of symbols vary to some extent from culture to culture, our shared experience as human beings – principally an experience of nature and of the human life-cycle – has generated a universal language of symbolism. Because motifs such as a tree, a flower, water, fire, sun and moon speak to people intuitively, regardless of race or creed, they offer great potential for exploration in healing. It is these signs that form the basis of many of the mandalas in this book.

In addition there is the symbolic geometry of the mandala, and this too is universal: the circle is universally endless, the triangle always suggests a flame, the square always signifies the created world. Other, more culturally rooted symbols used in these pages – the Egyptian Eye of Horus, the Sanskrit *Om* symbol, the *I-Ching* hexagrams of China – have an intrinsic beauty and long-lived significance that endows them with a universal potency.

On pages 36–46 you will find a series of commentaries on many of the symbols you will find in the mandalas. Further information on specific symbols is given in the meditations that accompany the thirty mandalas, and on the feature pages (with quotations) that punctuate these meditations. Each time you meditate on the mandalas, keep your mind open to the full range of possible interpretations. One image can carry a number of associations – the rose, for example, can stand for love, beauty and compassion. Your response to a motif at

SYMBOLIC ARCHITECTURE

A church, temple or chapel can serve as a three-dimensional mandala, with symbolic geometry and motifs all around. Such buildings have healing potential for those who use them as a sanctuary for body, mind and spirit.

Dome Symbolically, the dome is either the cosmos or the heavens. Any light that enters is the light of spiritual wisdom.

Stupa This type of Buddhist temple is structured to symbolize the five elements. Its square base represents earth; its hemispherical dome, water; and its conical spire, fire. The crescent moon finial signifies air; its circular disk, space.

Cross The vertical and horizontal axes of a cross represent the potential for spirit and matter to meet, as well as the redemptive possibilities of human suffering.

Mesoamerican pyramid Some stepped temples in Central America are models of the cosmos. Often, the north side of their square plan represents the underworld; the south side, life and rebirth.

any moment will reflect not only your worldview, your cultural background and your knowledge, but also your changing moods. This aspect of variability adds depth to mandala meditation and enlarges its healing potential.

GEOMETRIC SHAPES

Geometry is a key element in mandala symbolism. The mind is drawn to geometric shapes, which, as objects of meditation, help to establish a positive framework for our thoughts. Free of explicit representational content, geometry has a purity that enables it to work well as a mental resting place. Yet at the same time, it can be rich in implications. It offers ways of visualizing, for example, the interaction of spirit and flesh (the cross) or the concept of eternity (the circle).

The circle In the circle, we experience perfect symmetry, integrity, unity and completeness, and beyond those qualities, a visual equivalent of eternity. In mandalas, the basic circle shape is emblematic of the spiritual, in contrast to the earthly square. As a ring, the endlessness of the circle signifies commitment: a promise never to falter. Interlocking circles make this promise mutual.

The spiral A common form in nature (think of the snail's shell, for example), the continuous curves of the spiral symbolize a cyclical and progressive

Right: Spirals, often found in shells (this is a Moon Snail shell), may occur in mandalas.

They symbolize our deepening understanding as we spiral into our own inner selves.

continuity. The spiral suggests our inner growth as we move onward and inward in our wide-ranging explorations of our own consciousness.

The central point The central point of a mandala, traditionally known in Sanskrit as the *bindu*, stands for our own awareness as we start our meditation. Everything begins and ends with this dot, which is both seed and bud. It is the point at which the self recognizes its identity with the One.

The square This shape stands for Earth as opposed to Heaven, though it can also imply the solid, created universe as distinct from the transcendent creator, the One. The square also suggests a pause or breathing space.

The cross This is the most complex of all linear symbols. It is both the emblem of Christianity and a more ancient image of the cosmos reduced to its simplest terms – two intersecting lines indicating four directions, the cardinal points. The cross is also a simplification of the Tree of Life, its vertical axis suggesting spiritual ascension and its horizontal axis earthly life.

The triangle This ancient symbol of wisdom and spirit may suggest spiritual energy flowing into the physical world. Equilateral triangles in a mandala encourage in the viewer a reassuring sense of unity. The three points of a triangle reminds us of a trinity – humanity, God and spirit, or perhaps earth, sea and sky. (For interlocking triangles, see **The star**, page 40.)

NUMBER SYMBOLISM

The components of mandalas are often repeated, and when they are, there tends to be hidden symbolism in their numerical meaning. Philosophers and mathematicians of the ancient world, such as Plato, Pythagoras, Archimedes and Euclid, recognized the symbolic significance of numbers and ascribed sacred meanings to them. You might not consciously feel these connections as you meditate on a mandala, but often the number will feel relevant and carry weight.

1 A reminder of your singularity (your indivisible perfection) as well as of unity – the lack of differentiation between you and the cosmos.

2 Symbolizes duality, and also the division of the cosmos into opposites, such as male/female, light/dark, yin/yang and internal/external. The number may call you to balance and harmony.

3 The most positive of numbers, implying synthesis, growth, creativity.

4 Four components in a mandala may suggest stability, the earth, justice. They can offer a reassuring sense of working within boundaries.

5 Echoes the human form, with its four limbs and head, and five senses. This number may point at the power of individuality and spiritual aspirations.

6 Represents balance and symmetry, while doubling the creative energy of the number three.

7 A sacred, mystical and magical number, symbolizing cosmic and spiritual order, and the completion of a cycle or series (days of the week, number of chakras).

8 Can evoke a sensation of solidity, and double the qualities of the number four.

9 A triple triad, considered to be a very powerful number, symbolizing completion, fulfilment and the attainment of spiritual heights.

The star A star may be a five-pointed pentacle (comprising a continuous line) or a six-pointed hexagram (two interlocking triangles, one inverted in relation to the other). The pentacle, as the Star of Solomon, is a symbol of health and mystic harmony. The hexagram symbolizes union in duality (body/soul, male/female, and so on). More straightforwardly, a shining star, with alternating long and short points, is an auspicious sign and a spiritual centre.

NATURE'S LEXICON

Nature is a source of inspiration and value. We treasure those phenomena of the cosmos that are independent of humankind. We find beauty and profundity when we lose ourselves in the contemplation of life-forms that are beyond rational understanding. In mandalas, the deeply symbolic associations of plants, and sometimes animals, speak to us at a level that transcends cultural differences. To some extent, a tree or a flower has general significance related to nature's cycles, while animals tend to represent the Other, a self that is emphatically not our own. But when we consider individual families or species of plants or animals, a more individual symbolism comes into play – for example, the association of pine trees, in Japanese tradition, with longevity, or the cat, in Western tradition, with instinctive pliability and subtlety.

Trees With their roots in the soil and their branches in the sky, trees inhabit both earthly and heavenly realms: they are antennae for spiritual energy from above, yet remain firmly anchored in the created world. Their roots draw sustenance from an underground water supply, reminding us that we may need to dig deep at times to access our nourishment. The trunk, especially of the oak, symbolizes solidity and strength, while the agility of the willow's more flexible stem reminds us that we are capable of more than we might imagine and can weather storms if we bend with the wind. Branches reach aspiringly toward the spiritual realm, and blossom reminds us that our spiritual ambitions may be realized in a beautiful flowering, but that this soon will pass.

Flowers Though short-lived – a symbol of our impermanence – flowers remind us of the inner beauty that will flourish if we conduct ourselves well in thought and deed. The lotus has a rich symbolism in the East. Its power comes from the beauty of its radiating petals, said to represent an idealized form of the vulva, the blessed source of life – hence a link with birth, rebirth and the creator gods. Also, because the lotus rises from mud to open immaculate petals to the sun, it stands for our spiritual growth from base matter to the soul's divine perfection. No less significant is the rose, a mystical symbol of the heart, hub of the cosmic wheel – though in the Christian tradition it also denotes sacrifice.

Multi-layered rose petals suggest spiritual initiation. To deepen the mystic significance of the rose it may be laid over a cross, in which case its symbolic meanings multiply dizzyingly. The chrysanthemum, which is the imperial and solar flower of Japan, is associated with longevity. Other flowers, of course, have healing significance in the long-established tradition of herbalism.

Animals Creatures, both real and mythical, can be read as elements of our instinctive nature – an antidote to over-sophistication yet dangerous if allowed to revert to a selfish pursuit of bestial appetites. Beyond this there are specific meanings. The phoenix's transformative powers urge us to burn off unwanted attachments and find rebirth in a new self-awareness. The dragon (in its Eastern incarnations) offers us a model for regenerative energy through its association with rain-bringing thunder (often shown as a pearl in the dragon's mouth). The lion, with its golden coat and radiant mane, is a powerful incarnation of the sun.

Birds In mandalas, birds generally suggest transcendence. The dove is a familiar emblem of peace, purity, love, tenderness and hope. The eagle, soaring in the realm of spirit, and looking down on the world, evokes clarity of vision. The crane, sacred in the East, suggests longevity, wisdom and fidelity. The owl, more obviously, represents far-sighted wisdom. The peacock, shimmeringly majestic, denotes immortality, solar glory, incorruptibility and self-worth.

READING THE ELEMENTS

The Western tradition recognizes four elements – earth, fire, air and water – corresponding to the four seasons. In the Chinese tradition, however, there is also a fifth season, with its own element: ether, spirit or space. When your eye rests upon motifs that represent the elements or seasons in a mandala, you begin to tap into their energies, which can help to bring body and mind toward greater equilibrium in much the same way that spending time in nature is restorative.

Earth Usually represented as mountains, rocks, soil or grass, earth in a mandala reminds us of the material, practical part of our lives. It may allude to healing the body and issues to do with work and possessions. Earth is linked to the north and to winter, the season of recuperative withdrawal and dormancy.

Air Depicted as blowing leaves or clouds, air in a mandala stands for the mind, and the far-carrying power of thought. Air is the medium of communication, which may be the clue to healing. This element is linked to the east and spring, a time of fresh growth and new beginnings.

Fire Flame-like motifs stand for fire, the source of spirit, inspiration and passion, as well as action and enthusiasm. Fire's healing action is cleansing and transformative: it destroys unwanted clutter, creating space for the new. Fire links to the south and summer, when energy is highest.

Water This ebbing and flowing element symbolizes the emotions. Often it takes a moving form: rivers, waterfalls, oceans, teardrops. Water shapes itself to the container that holds it, reminding us to be flexible. It is linked to the west and autumn, a time of gathering and preparation.

Ether Sometimes shown as the sky, ether urges us to look for the spiritual source, beyond form. Also, it is set at the hub of the wheel of the elements and seasons, which magnifies its healing potency.

COSMIC SYMBOLS

Images of heavenly bodies in mandalas remind us to expand our horizons from individual concerns by looking out toward the vast, awesome universe.

The cosmos makes us feel small when we contemplate its immeasurable magnitude, yet in fact this immensity is part of ourselves, and the cosmos is very much our home. By meditating on mandalas we can feel this sense of belonging even as we start more fully to comprehend the sublime vastness of the universe. Similarly, we are connected to all other people by a powerful bond of spirit. Our

---

TRADITIONAL MANDALA SYMBOLISM

The following traditional figures can be found depicted in the mandalas that a lot of us are most familiar with: those of the Buddhist faith.

Healing Buddha Featured in diverse forms in different traditions, the Healing Buddha embodies the state of enlightenment, and liberation from the cycle of birth and rebirth. By gazing on him, we reconnect with our own Buddha-like nature, which is untroubled by the material world.

The goddess of compassion In Tibet, Tara is the female embodiment of the Buddha and represents unconditional love and compassion. Green Tara and White Tara are the forms most called upon for healing. In China, Tara appears as Kuan Yin.

Bodhisattvas These figures are enlightened beings who have chosen to remain in the material world to relieve the suffering of their fellow creatures. They remind us that spiritual hope and comfort are there for us in times of need if only we can be receptive.

separateness is an illusion: we are deeply in harmony with – indeed, continuous with – everyone and everything. Mandalas reconnect us with this truth.

Sun, moon and stars help us to apprehend our connection with the cosmos by forming a bridge between cosmic reality and human experience. The sun is incomprehensibly distant yet directly controls the seasons. All physical energy comes from the sun, making it apt as a symbol of spiritual energy, an analogy for divinity itself. And the moon, with its monthly phases, is emblematic of change and renewal in nature and in human life, as well as having connotations of mystic wisdom, intuition and the feminine. The stars, less precisely, suggest the ineffable wonder of creation, spiritual aspiration and the promise of transcendence.

HUMAN AND HEAVENLY FORMS

Traditional mandalas often feature figures – especially deities (see box opposite) and demons. Where the Buddha appears in a mandala, he reminds us of the enlightenment that may be attained by following his principles of detachment from cravings, extinction of desire, and the key principles of right thinking, right action, right speech, right effort, right awareness and right concentration. In the Tibetan tantric tradition, the Buddha appears in female form as the goddess Tara, fount of unconditional love. Her protective action on behalf of all living beings is said to exceed that of a mother for her child. Green Tara is called upon in times of trouble and fear; White Tara, the "Mother of all Buddhas", is looked to as a source of compassion, purity, truth and unselfishness. Christians have their own equivalent of this feminine energy in the Virgin Mary.

In modern mandalas you might also encounter figures from the Greek and Roman pantheons – for example, Aphrodite or Venus for help in love or in creative pursuit; the centaur Chiron, tutor to gods and heroes, for healing inner and outer wounds; Mars for assertiveness; Mercury to foster communication.

HARMONY IN DUALITY

Mandala designs often include motifs that suggest a harmonious balance of opposites – most commonly the Chinese yin-yang symbol of interdependence, which features black and white areas within a circle, divided by an S-shaped curve. Each area of the symbol includes a dot, or seed, of its opposite colour to show that the duality of light/dark, male/female, logic/intuition is not absolute: instead, there is a balanced dynamism, an interdependence of contrary forces within the cosmos. The yang contains the energy of the yin, and vice versa. Creative tension between the two generates change and motion, and gives texture and colour to our life's experiences.

Right: This intricate sand mandala in Bhutan is carefully laid out by novice Buddhist monks. When it is complete, the mandala will be swept away, as a reminder of the impermanence of our existence.

As we meditate on the yin-yang symbol and allow the complementary opposites to filter into our consciousness, we absorb the intuition that happiness and sadness, good and bad times, doubt and belief, even illness and health, are necessary conditions of existence.

Spiritual teachers tell us that physical dualities are simply diverse expressions of the One – the unity and completeness that are the ultimate creative force, symbolized in a mandala by its outer circle and its central miniature dot. By absorbing the entire mandala in a single gaze at some time during our meditation, we can attune ourselves to cosmic harmony and drink in the sense of deep peace and unity that provides the foundation-stone for healing.

WORKING WITH THIS BOOK

There are 30 mandalas in this book, each complete with a step-by-step meditation. They are grouped in three sections: *Finding The Whole Self*, *The Self and Others* and *The Self in Times of Challenge*. It is hoped that these categories are self-explanatory, but there is inevitably, of course, a great deal of overlap: when the overall aim is holistic, it is counterproductive to insist on divisions.

Within each section, the mandalas are arranged in no particular order: there is no progression from one to another, just as there is no definitive way to interpret their motifs. It is entirely up to you how you decide which mandala to start with, and which ones to work on thereafter. Bearing in mind that it is chiefly your unconscious mind that absorbs and processes the symbols, motifs and colours within an image, it can be helpful to be guided by your intuition when deciding which mandala most suits your current needs. Just select one that appeals really strongly to you. Your choice may change each time you return to the book, or you may opt to work with one mandala for a while. Go with whatever has resonance for you. On the other hand, by all means feel free to choose a mandala on the strength of its title or the chapter in which it falls, especially if you have come to the book to resolve a problem.

Mandala meditation can feel like the ancient spiritual tradition of walking a labyrinth, which, as you progress, takes you deeper into the realms of the self. For each of the mandalas there is step-by-step guidance to help you on this journey toward your still centre. You can follow these guidelines word for word or simply view them as a reassuring presence to return to when you feel a little lost in your self-exploration. The text guidance may help you to focus on the images and open your mind to some of their symbolism. As previously stated, however, you should aim, eventually, to work without these guidelines, approaching the image only with a still, clear mind and a trust in your intuition.

Each time you meditate on a mandala, you will experience new insights, and these will become more profound as you strip away layers of conditioned thinking. If you find yourself disturbed by any particular image or thought that occurs to you, just call a halt to that meditation: it may not be right for you at this time. Perhaps it is asking you to look at issues you are not yet ready to confront on your healing journey. Come back to meditate on another mandala whenever you feel ready. These mandalas will always be there for you.

To guide your explorations and provide a refreshing interlude, some of the thirty mandalas are followed by an extra feature that expands on one of the symbols or themes you will have just encountered. There are inspiring quotations from classic and modern texts – and you might choose to meditate on these words now and then, as a change from the visual work. Some of the extra features include practical suggestions of various kinds, taking your journey outside this book and continuing it by other means. Often you will be given insights into traditional symbolism, or you will be encouraged to think in new ways about everyday phenomena.

To conclude, we offer on the opposite page a practical step-by-step procedure for working with this book that may be helpful to those who are meditating on a mandala for the first time.

MANDALA MEDITATION BASICS

Although the meditations in this book are simple and need no further guidance to be effective, at first the discipline of sitting to meditate may seem a little daunting. However, if you persevere, it can soon become second nature. It helps if you set aside a particular time for meditation each day, perhaps on waking or before bed. At first, meditate for ten minutes, building up to 15 or 20 minutes.

1 Find a quiet, warm place where you will not be disturbed. Sit comfortably on the floor with your legs crossed and a firm cushion beneath your buttocks, or on a chair with your feet flat on the floor and your lower back well supported.

2 Place your chosen mandala at eye level in front of you, a little more than arm's length away. Then settle yourself and rest your hands in your lap, fingers interlinked with palms facing upward.

3 Take some deep, calming breaths, then begin to look at the mandala. Your eyes may flicker from one element to another at first. Allow this to happen, but when you feel ready, soften your gaze a little and look at the whole image for a minute or two.

4 Then let your eyes slowly follow the progression of patterns and symbols, letting each symbol enter your mind and sit there, working its mysterious effect. Either follow the step-by-step meditation given or explore freely — or a mixture of the two. Try not to interpret the motifs or colours, nor to analyze your thoughts as they occur. Just let the mandala journey inside you: absorb its patterns and allow its symbols to soak into your awareness.

5 If at any time you find your eyes darting around and your mind becoming restless, take a deep breath, consciously slow down, and reconnect with a state of relaxation.

6 When you feel ready to finish, close your eyes and sit quietly for a few moments to allow your body and mind to digest the experience. Then, wriggle your fingers; stretch to reconnect with your body. And write down any impressions you are left with — later you can consider what they mean.

FINDING THE WHOLE SELF

The ten mandalas that follow give you routes toward your still centre. You can use them to draw emotional and spiritual sustenance from your inner wellspring. Spending time with these mandalas brings healing from the inside out as you boost your self-esteem, learn to recognize your inner beauty and strength, enhance your creative expression, confront your fears and embrace change. Wholeness, peace and wisdom are within your reach.

SPIRAL OF LIFE

WE ARE ALL CHILDREN OF THE COSMOS. THE MOLECULES THAT MAKE UP THE PHYSICAL

SELF ARE FOUND UNIVERSALLY: WE ARE ALL ONE. SENSING THE COSMIC LIFE-ENERGY

WE SHARE ALLOWS US TO GIVE BIRTH TO EVER NEW FACETS OF OURSELVES, SO THAT

WE BECOME MORE WHOLE. THIS IS THE ESSENCE OF HEALING.

1 Rest your gaze on the embryo in the protective egg at the centre of the mandala — a symbol of new life and potential. Feel cradled in the confidence that there are infinite possibilities for future growth.

2 Now let your eyes find the spirals of gold around the baby. Their shape is a reminder that life moves in cycles, and that we are all engaged in constant change and growth.

3 Next, focus on the twisting strands of DNA that define all the features of your unique self. Imagine some of these transforming into strands of pearls — or wisdom.

4 Finally, bathe in the vibrant blue of boundless space and inner potential, and trace the perfect circle enclosing this place of wonder. Feel no fear. You are safe here to express all the aspects of your true nature.

> *Life is the soul's nursery —*
> *its training place for the destinies of eternity.*
>
> **WILLIAM MAKEPEACE THACKERAY (1811–1863)**

SELF IN THE COSMOS

EVERYTHING BEGINS WITH THE SELF. ALTHOUGH EACH OF US IS BUT A SPECK IN THE COSMOS, ONCE WE REALIZE OUR CONNECTIONS WITH EVERYTHING THAT IS, AND THAT THERE ARE NO LIMITS TO OUR CONTRIBUTION, WE GAIN A SENSE OF SELF-WORTH AND PURPOSE THAT NOURISHES OUR WELL-BEING.

1 Let your eyes rest on the centre of the mandala and its vibrant pentacle, a symbol of the wonder of life and of self-realization. Imagine that the power of its sacred geometry is flowing into you.

2 Look at the floating figure: this is one of us and all of us. It is you, and all the others with whom you share a bond of cosmic kinship. You are bestride the universe.

3 Next, transfer your attention to the flowers. Let the natural cycles they symbolize bathe you in purity (snowdrops), hope and renewal (daffodils), love (roses), self-truth (chrysanthemums) and protection (peonies).

4 Finally, let the stars at the periphery call your attention to the beautiful truth of creation. Each shining star is unique, despite being one of millions. So are you.

> *The universe is transformation;*
> *our life is what our thoughts make it.*

MARCUS AURELIUS (121–180 CE)

A FLOWER FOR ALL SEASONS

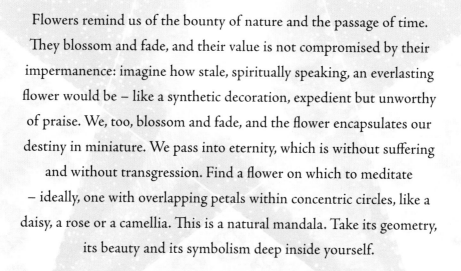

Flowers remind us of the bounty of nature and the passage of time.
They blossom and fade, and their value is not compromised by their
impermanence: imagine how stale, spiritually speaking, an everlasting
flower would be – like a synthetic decoration, expedient but unworthy
of praise. We, too, blossom and fade, and the flower encapsulates our
destiny in miniature. We pass into eternity, which is without suffering
and without transgression. Find a flower on which to meditate
– ideally, one with overlapping petals within concentric circles, like a
daisy, a rose or a camellia. This is a natural mandala. Take its geometry,
its beauty and its symbolism deep inside yourself.

....

FLOWER POWER

"If we could see the miracle of a single flower clearly,
our whole life would change."

THE BUDDHA (C.563–C.483 BCE)

SOUL FOOD

"Bread feeds the body, indeed,
but flowers feed also the soul."

THE PROPHET MUHAMMAD (569–632 CE)

ETERNAL OM

OM IS THE SACRED SYLLABLE REPRESENTING THE SOUND THAT BROUGHT CREATION

INTO BEING — THE DIVINE WORD. CREATIVE ENERGY IS THE SOURCE OF EVERYTHING.

IN OUR OWN LIVES, IT UNDERLIES ALL OUR PERCEPTIONS. WE ARE NOT PASSIVE,

WE ARE PROFOUNDLY ACTIVE. OUR TRUE SELF CAN WORK ITS OWN MIRACLES.

1 Let your gaze settle on the golden *OM* (in Sanskrit) at the centre of this mandala. Let this symbol of creative force connect you with your own, ever-present creative energy.

2 Move your eyes outward to the Star of David, a meeting of two triangles. Their intertwining resembles the mixing within yourself of the mortal and the divine. Dwell here for a moment, aware of the connections.

3 Next, shift your gaze to the white birds within the points of the star. They stand for your freedom to express yourself, and the joy that this brings. Let yourself relax and experience a liberating sensation of flying.

4 Fly with the birds toward the flames — the fires of imagination and passion waiting to transform thoughts into action. Feel the pride of being true to your creative self.

> *The possible's slow fuse is lit by the imagination.*

EMILY DICKINSON (1830–1886)

LOOK SKYWARD

"When thou seest an eagle,
thou seest a portion of genius; lift up thy head."

WILLIAM BLAKE (1757–1827)

DANCE, THEN FLY

"It is no doubt possible to fly — but first you must
know how to dance like an angel."

FRIEDRICH NIETZSCHE (1844–1900)

FREEDOM IN FLIGHT

It is hard to imagine life without birds. Their song is nature singing its own anthem, and their flight is a glorious reminder of our own best aspirations and of our deepest self – free and soulful. Birds also represent messages from the divine. They are mediators, moving freely between physical and spiritual worlds, as the human mind can when it shakes off its attachments and cares. In the *Upanishads*, two birds in the Cosmic Tree, one eating and one watching, represent the individual and the universal soul. Meditate on this image. Visualize also the dove with the olive branch heralding dry land for Noah as the Flood waters recede. Dry land would be sterile without birds.

MOONLIGHT 4 EPIPHANY

IF WE LISTEN TO OUR INTUITION — OUR WISE INNER VOICE — IT CAN LEAD US ALONG
A HEALING PATH THAT IS APPROPRIATE FOR EACH OF US RIGHT NOW. WE CAN
EXPERIENCE INTUITION AS FLASHES OF INSIGHT, VIVID DREAMS OR A SENSE OF
DEEP RECOGNITION. TUNE INTO AND TRUST THESE IRRATIONAL PERCEPTIONS.

1 Pass through the outer circle of the mandala, the rim of the moon — a gateway to the unconscious and the intuitive realm of profound understanding and truth.

2 Now bring your gaze inward, to the centre of the mandala, and to the river flowing smoothly around rocks. Go with the flow: imagine yourself dodging obstacles to your well-being with ease.

3 Notice the silvery fish, signs of wisdom, leaping from the water. Open yourself to the wise ideas jumping from your unconscious.

4 Move upstream toward the river's source, a well-spring of self-healing. Allow your eyes to be drawn toward the hills, subtly shaped like a sleeping woman, a sign of latent intuition. Even in sleep the moon and stars shine down, revealing where the wise self lies.

"I have given you words of vision and wisdom ... Ponder them in the silence of your soul, and then in freedom do your will."

BHAGAVAD GITA (1ST OR 2ND CENTURY BCE)

MOON MAGIC

As ancient peoples gazed at the changing moon, they wove stories about how, each month, the orb was devoured by animals or gods, then miraculously renewed. The moon's phases therefore gave rise to associations with the cycle of birth, life and death, while its dark side stood for the hidden psyche. Devise your own lunar healing ceremonies. Anchor your intentions for self-growth to the new and waxing moon, gaze at the full moon to recharge your energies, shed negative thoughts as the moon wanes. Think about the intertidal shore, which would not have existed were it not for moon-driven tides. This is where amphibious life began. We are all amphibious in having one foot in the flesh, one foot in the spirit.

REVELATION

"The moon abiding
In the midst of a tranquil mind;
Clouds break into light."

DOGEN (1200–1253)

GATEWAY TO THE HEART

"The silver light, which, hallowing tree and tower,
Sheds beauty and deep softness o'er the whole,
Breathes also to the heart."

LORD BYRON (1788–1824)

THE UNFOLDING NOW

THERE IS ONLY NOW — THOUGH, OF COURSE, THE MOMENT ELUDES US AS SOON AS WE PAUSE TO NOTICE IT. IF WE CAN FULLY UNDERSTAND HOW MOMENT BY MOMENT WE EXPERIENCE THE NOW OF NATURE, WHICH IS THE SAME NOW EXPERIENCED (NOT MENTALLY, OF COURSE) BY TREES AND FLOWERS, WE GRASP A SUBSTANTIAL TRUTH.

1 Bring your gaze to the cross of silhouetted figures. Feel the vibrant energy streaming toward you from the coloured chakra centres on the four bodies. Breathe in the power and potential of this unfolding present moment.

2 Follow the coloured chakras to the crown of each head. They are so balanced and in tune with now that serpentine energy spills over from one moment into the next.

3 Now find the outstretched arms embracing each moment and stretching out to the trees. Imagine your awareness and senses opening right now like buds so that you can draw in the oaks' strength and the acorns' potential.

4 Finally, let your gaze settle on the point at which the human and tree trunks merge, grounded in the moment. Absorbing strength and balance, simply be here, now.

> *Now. This is it. The whole purpose and meaning for the existence of everything.*
>
> **ZEN SAYING**

HEALING 6 MOTION

WHEN YOU EMBRACE RATHER THAN RESIST CHANGE, YOU BEGIN TO LIVE WITH A

FLUIDITY THAT FREES UP YOUR ENERGIES FOR HEALTHY LIVING. THIS MANDALA,

INCORPORATING TRIGRAMS (AS PRESENTED IN THE *I CHING*, OR *BOOK OF CHANGES*),

CARRIES YOU INTO THE FUTURE ON STREAMS OF EVER-CHANGING ENERGY.

1 Start with your gaze at the centre of the mandala, where the wheel of the year emerges from a spiral of light. Sense time unrolling around you, moment after moment, bringing with it the potential for change.

2 Let your eyes rest on the elements you need to grasp to ground yourself in changing creation: solid earth, the air of the higher realms, inner fire and ever-flowing water.

3 Now look at the three-line trigrams against their turquoise background. See how their varying short and longer lines ring the changes on a world of potential. Allow the possibilities they symbolize to permeate deep into your being.

4 Picture the eight-pointed star bursting forth, a dynamo of power whose structure holds ever firm while it pulses out light.

They must often change, who would be constant in happiness or wisdom.

CONFUCIUS (551–479 BCE)

CASTING CHANGES

The *I Ching*, or *Book of Changes*, is a classical Chinese text made up
of a system of symbols used to make predictions and offer advice.
It is based on the eight trigram symbols shown in the mandala on page
71. Each is an arrangement of solid (yang) and broken (yin) lines.
Symbolized in this is the Taoist belief that the cosmos is based on
a constant flux of complementary forces. The trigrams are combined
to form 64 possible hexagrams. To cast the *I Ching*, you throw yarrow
sticks – like throwing dice. Chance, it is implied, is never random:
it aligns itself to the grain of our destiny. This does not impede free
will, but simply means that no event is without significance.

EVER MOVING FORWARD

"Keeping adding, keep walking, keep advancing."

ST AUGUSTINE (354–430)

UNIVERSAL TRUTH

"All things change; nothing perishes."

OVID (43 BCE–17 CE)

JEWEL IN THE LOTUS

IN EASTERN TRADITIONS, THE LOTUS IS A SYMBOL OF THE UNSULLIED HEART OR SOUL,

RISING FROM THE MUDDY WATERS OF HUMAN IMPERFECTIONS. OUR INNER BEAUTY,

ONCE WE NOURISH IT, BLOSSOMS TO REVEAL ASTONISHING PURITY. REVEAL THIS

BEAUTY TO THE OUTSIDE WORLD LIKE THE LOTUS OPENING TO THE SUN.

1 Rest your eyes on the luminous diamond unfolded by the lotus. It represents the value of your hidden depths and an invincible strength born from pressure.

2 Now contemplate the petals themselves. They show the beauty of your generous soul, a flowering of love — strength, giving, compassion and beauty fused.

3 Shift your gaze to the rising sun behind the diamond and lotus — the eternal divine that inspires the divine in ourselves to emerge.

4 Finally, find the halo of pearls — wisdom through experience. Let their gentle sheen be a reflection of the inner beauty shining out from you. They give you self-esteem and a protective outer ring of many virtues.

> *Though we travel the world over to find the beautiful,*
> *we must carry it with us, or we find it not.*

RALPH WALDO EMERSON (1803–1882)

LOOK WITHIN

"Many individuals have, like uncut diamonds, shining qualities beneath a rough exterior."

JUVENAL (LATE 1ST/EARLY 2ND CENTURY CE)

SMOOTHING THE SOUL

"The soul is placed in the body like a rough diamond, and must be polished, or the lustre of it will never appear."

DANIEL DEFOE (1660—1731)

ENDURING BRILLIANCE

Diamonds have been revered since antiquity. The ancient Greeks believed that they were the tears of the gods, while the Romans considered them to be fragments of falling stars. The extraordinary physical properties of the diamond – the world's hardest material – make it an apt symbol of enduring love, purity, strength, courage and indestructibility. Within Eastern spiritual teachings, this gemstone is also used as an analogy of the soul, which endures through countless incarnations with its purity of intention untarnished. Diamonds are said to open a portal to spiritual growth. Sit quietly and meditate on the qualities of a diamond if you cannot afford to wear one.

RIPPLING  WATERS

WATER CAN SOOTHE THE MIND: GAZING AT THE VASTNESS OF THE OCEAN IN ALL ITS

MOODS PUTS WORRIES INTO PERSPECTIVE, WHILE LOOKING INTO A STILL LAKE OR

POND CAN GUIDE US INTO A RELAXED STATE IN WHICH WE CAN EXPERIENCE TRUE

INSIGHT AND SHED ILLUSIONS WITHOUT PANIC.

1 Look into the centre of the mandala, at the flower-head floating on the surface of a deep pool. Imagine you yourself are floating, in air rather than in water, as you look down into the depths. You feel safe and relaxed.

2 Now gaze into the pool as it ripples in circles. A wind is stirring its surface, but down below lies deep calm. Let its tranquillity permeate deep inside you.

3 Now bring your attention to the willow leaves overhanging the pool's edges. They are firmly connected to the bank yet flourish in the air. Your inner stillness shares their grounded flexibility.

4 Lastly, take in the mandala as a whole with its border of pebbles and flowers and its lily-pad corners. Feel its ripples spread through your mind in an endless flow.

If water derives clarity from stillness, how much more so does the mind!

ZHUANGZI (C.369–286 BCE)

WILD-HORSE WINDS

THE HORSE IS A FASCINATING ANIMAL — STRANGELY HUMAN IN ITS INTELLIGENCE

AND ITS CAPACITY FOR WORK, YET TOTALLY OTHER IN ITS FOUR-LEGGED FORM. HERE,

WE CONNECT WITH ITS HEALING FORCE, MAGNIFIED BY THE WINDS OF CHANGE.

LEAP WITH THESE HORSES TO FREEDOM AND WELL-BEING.

1 Find the vortex of energy at the mandala's centre, where a wind is rising. Watch it spin a spiral of leaves and let this blow away your anxieties. The brown leaves signify all you have outgrown, and green is for regeneration.

2 Now gaze at the galloping horses, feeling your energy increase, and past fears fall away. Embrace the horses' freedom. Trust them: they in turn will trust you and your kindness.

3 Expand your awareness to the ring of laurel leaves, traditionally used to crown a great poet. In so doing, you discover the poetry of your own spirit.

4 Finally, look at the grounding shape of interlocking squares, and the broken chains in its corners. Mentally sever your connection with everything that holds you back and enjoy the healing sense of release this brings.

"When you ... are unable to control your mind, your senses do not obey you, just as unruly horses do not obey a charioteer."

UPANISHADS (C.1000 BCE)

BLOWING IN THE WIND

*"… since the wind blows in my face,
I sail with every wind."*

FRIEDRICH NIETZSCHE (1844–1900)

THE NATURE OF CHANGE

*"Change is the nursery of music, joy, life
and eternity."*

JOHN DONNE (1572–1631)

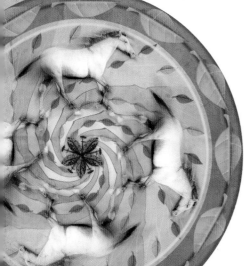

THE WINDS OF CHANGE

Being outside on a windy day is exhilarating. We feel the energy of
nature, and it can seem as if our cobwebs of anxiety, depression or
tiredness are being blown away by a force that finds them irrelevant – a
force seen and heard, yet invisible in itself. Wind is cousin to air and to
breath, hence the importance of its symbolism. It clears us of clutter,
lifts our spirits and rearranges the familiar. A sailing ship without wind
would be as useless as a body without a soul, or a human being without
a clear sense of their own destiny. Our wind chimes, which tell us that
life is change, are all around us: listen to the rustling of leaves whenever
you can, for there was never a truer word spoken.

TRIPLE SPIRAL

THE INTERLOCKING CURLICUES OF A TRIPLE SPIRAL ILLUSTRATE THE WHOLENESS OF

MIND, SPIRIT AND MATTER. IN THE UNION OF THE TRINITY, THE MEETING OF EARTH,

WATER AND SKY, THE INTERTWINING OF PAST, PRESENT AND FUTURE, WE FIND MODELS

FOR THE INTEGRATED SELF, WHICH GAINS UNDERSTANDING BY SPIRAL PROGRESSION.

1 Let your gaze rest on the entire mandala. Relax into the unity and completeness of all its elements. If you feel a sense of movement within the mandala, go with it. Feel how balance and movement co-exist.

2 Now focus on the large triple spiral and its central point, which represents your concentrated essence. Let your eyes trace the three distinct coils — mind, body and spirit.

Recall the spiral progress of your learning, spreading out from well-earned knowledge.

3 Move your gaze out to the beads threaded around the triple spiral. Each is separate and perfect, yet interconnects with the others to create a circle of beauty and harmony.

4 Finally, find the four shells in the corners. Even nature echoes the integrated self.

The gate of the soul will be flung wide open once complete harmony of the body, mind and spirit is attained.

INDIAN PROVERB

THE SELF
AND OTHERS

The ten mandalas that make up this chapter encourage you

to address and explore the relationships in your life – to open

your mind and find new ways of nurturing yourself through

peace-making, forgiveness and accepting differences. They do

so indirectly, by asking your mind to become quiet and dwell

on symbolic resonances. These mandalas allow your intuition

to suggest ways to heal conflict and restore loving connections.

RAINBOW UNION

EACH OF US HAS A DUAL NATURE: MASCULINE AND FEMININE, ACTIVE AND RECEPTIVE,

AND REASON AND INTUITION COEXIST WITHIN US. BALANCING THESE SEEMINGLY

POLAR ENERGIES WITHIN OURSELVES IS A HEALING EXPERIENCE THAT EQUIPS US FOR

AN INNER DIALOGUE WITH A LIFE PARTNER WHOSE QUALITIES COMPLEMENT OURS.

1 Pour your gaze into the golden chalice, vessel of your feminine qualities. Now focus on the sword of determination, symbol of your masculine energy. Sense these opposites move toward each other at the centre of the mandala — reflecting their potential to come together within yourself and your relationship.

2 Now look at the interlinked male/female signs. They represent your true dual nature.

Feel intuition and reason merging in a union you can both celebrate.

3 Trace the repeating "lemniscates" — the figures of eight that reach out to connect male and female signs into perfect harmony.

4 Finally, seek out the rainbows, whose colours echo those of your chakras. They bless the union of opposites.

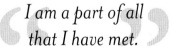

*I am a part of all
that I have met.*

ALFRED, LORD TENNYSON (1809–1892)

LANGUAGE OF COLOUR

"Mere colour, unspoiled by meaning and unallied with definite form, can speak to the soul in a thousand different ways."

OSCAR WILDE (1854–1900)

BE THOU THE RAINBOW

"Be thou the rainbow in the storms of life. The evening beam that smiles the clouds away, and tints tomorrow with prophetic ray."

LORD BYRON (1788–1824)

A HEALING SPECTRUM

The mystical beauty of a rainbow comes from the prism created by
droplets of water in the air following rain. Its harmonious colours
remind us that when life's storms pass, there can, once again, be peace
if we believe in it and look for it. The rainbow is a universal symbol
of interdependency, as well as a bridge between the earthly realm and
the unseen. In the body, its seven colours are associated with the major
chakras, from red at the base to violet at the crown. When you see a
rainbow, let it remind you to look for the beauty of the soul within. But
think too of the "rainbow nation" – the ideal of a peaceful mixed society
that depends on enlightened people passing on their wisdom.

HEALING MIRROR

TWO HANDS THAT COME TOGETHER IN A GESTURE OF PRAYER FOR OTHERS CAN

CHANGE THE WORLD — BY REJECTING SELFISHNESS AND SPREADING COMPASSION.

THESE ARE HANDS THAT COULD BE BUSY IN ACQUISITIVE ACTIVITY, BUT INSTEAD THEY

STOP AND PERFORM A SELFLESS CEREMONY.

1 Rest your gaze on the yin-yang symbol in the centre of the mandala. See how each half envelops an element of the other. Appreciate the dynamic union of the pairing.

2 Now shift your attention to the pairs of reflected hands. See how, in their perfect mirror image, they denote not the vanity we often associate with mirrors but selfless prayer. The cross these pairs of hands

form symbolizes the perfect interfusion of humanity and divinity.

3 Widen your focus to take in the humming birds sipping from flowers — such is the succour given if we honour each other.

4 Finally, take in the perfectly reflected image in its entirety. Feel yourself effortlessly relaxing into a state of healing symmetry.

> *The heart of man is made to reconcile the most glaring contradictions.*
>
> **DAVID HUME (1711–1776)**

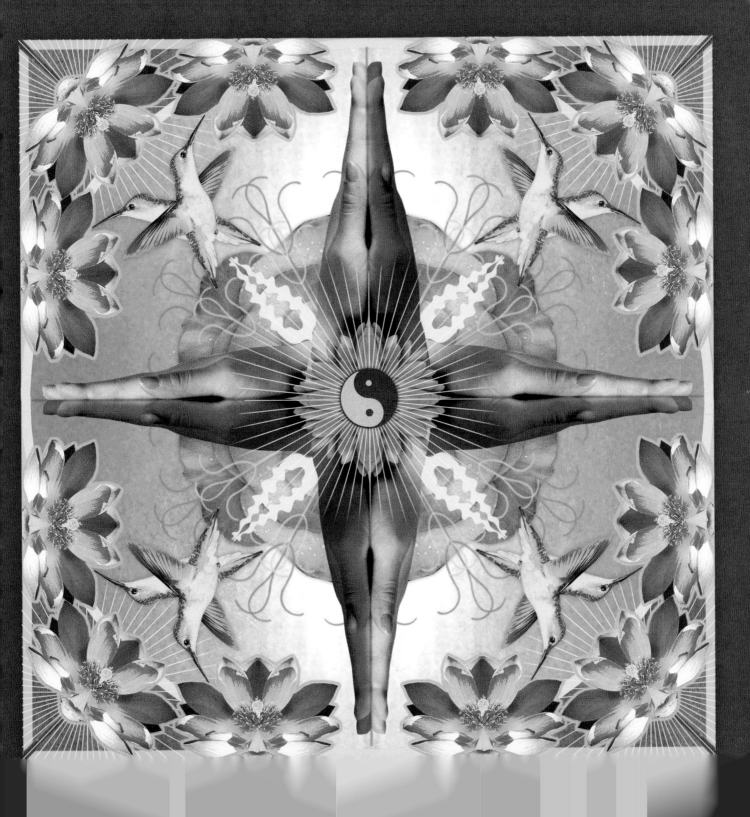

TWO TREES, ONE ROOT

TWO TREES SHARING ONE ROOT SYSTEM ARE A POTENT EXPRESSION OF INDEPENDENCE COMBINED WITH DEPENDENCE — A COMPLEX HARMONY. THIS MANDALA USES SUCH SYMBOLISM TO SHOW THE STRENGTH OF A HEALTHY RELATIONSHIP, MARRED BY NEITHER SERVILE WEAKNESS NOR OVERBEARING STRENGTH.

1 Take in the solid separateness of the twin tree trunks. Then turn to their canopy of leaves mingling in the air and their roots merging underground. Beyond the duality of individuals lies peaceful unity.

2 Contemplate the balances within the mandala: earth and air, yin and yang, light and shade. This mirrors the perfect meeting of body and mind and the pure connection — physical, mental and spiritual — between two people. Register this symbol, with its opposites, and let it rest in your consciousness.

3 Focus on the contrasting cranes. Imagine them crossing paths, exchanging positions and colours as they move through shadow and sunlight. Magical transformations take place when two people unite in harmony.

> " *Grow in each other's shade,*
> *and share the rain.* "

MAREO ALEMAN (1547–C.1609)

A DOME OVER ALL

THE IMAGE OF THE DOME, AS FOUND IN MANY PLACES OF WORSHIP OF DIFFERENT

FAITHS, REPRESENTS THE COSMOS BUT ALSO, LESS PRECISELY, THE POSSIBILITY OF

INTER-FAITH HARMONY IF ONLY SECTARIAN AND POLITICAL DIFFERENCES COULD BE

HEALED. THIS MANDALA INVOKES AND CELEBRATES THAT UTOPIAN VIEW.

1 Let your gaze rest on the eye in the centre of the mandala. Your wise self, this eye sits here as the "I" who witnesses and understands all without passing judgment.

2 Redirect *your* eyes to the frame through which this eye gazes — it looks out on four shining temples, each with its own dome. The mandala as a whole also represents a dome, seen in plan, with the heavens above.

3 Shift your gaze to the starry cosmos, in which no distinction of doctrine carries significance. Contrasting with the night, the golden dome shows the beauty that humankind can achieve, within themselves, when inspired by spirit rather than prejudice.

4 Finally, meditate on the eight soaring birds, symbolizing freedom of worship and proximity to the divine.

> *Life, like a dome of many-coloured glass,*
> *Stains the white radiance of Eternity.*

PERCY BYSSHE SHELLEY (1792–1822)

SACRED TEACHERS

As a privileged minority today in the West, we have the freedom
to choose our own faith by accepting or rejecting certain doctrines.
Hence we may come to believe in the One, the "power of now", loving-
kindness – and indeed mandala meditation. However, we should
never forget that the greatest thoughts humankind has had, about the
spirit and enlightenment, have come from individuals – wise ones who
have inspired not only by their words but also by their deeds. If you
happen to come across a good teacher, think yourself lucky and take
every opportunity to learn. Otherwise, read widely, think deeply and
remember that your latest thoughts are not necessarily your wisest.

THE PILLARS OF TRUTH

"Every truth has four corners. As a teacher I give you one corner, and it is for you to find the other three."

CONFUCIUS (551–479 BCE)

REVEALED KNOWLEDGE

"Jesus said: 'What is hidden from you will be disclosed to you … Split a piece of wood, I am there. Raise the stone, and you will find me there.'"

THE GOSPEL OF ST THOMAS (C.50–140 CE)

WINGS OF PEACE

THE BIBLICAL IMAGE OF THE DOVE CARRYING THE OLIVE BRANCH (SEE PAGE 103)

SUGGESTS NOT ONLY HOPE BUT ALSO RECONCILIATION — GOD MAKING PEACE WITH

THE WORLD. THIS MANDALA DEPLOYS BOTH SYMBOLS TO BRING PEACE INTO THE

HEART OF THE MEDITATOR AND HEAL A RIFT IN FRIENDSHIP OR LOVE.

1 Gaze at the flower unfolding in the centre of the mandala. Feel yourself relaxing into it. Sense yourself gradually blossoming into your natural state of peace — all enmity has withered away.

2 Fly with this peace on the wings of the doves. Lovely flowers bloom in peace's shadow. Imagine spreading loving wings around all who have hurt you.

3 Flying out into the world, you reach a circle of olive leaves. These are the hope that your peace will pacify others — it will if you believe it will.

4 Finally, gaze at the outer circle with its tiny flower-heads. Loving relationships with all, based on peace and forgiveness, nurture beauty in unexpected places. Be a gardener of love and beauty in the soil of peace.

> *First keep the peace within yourself,*
> *then you can also bring peace to others.*

THOMAS À KEMPIS (1380—1471)

AFTER THE FLOOD

"And the dove came in to him in the evening; and, lo, in her mouth was an olive leaf pluckt off: so Noah knew that the waters were abated from off the earth."

GENESIS 8.11

GENTLY, GENTLY

"Thoughts that come with doves' footsteps guide the world."

FRIEDRICH NIETZSCHE (1844—1900)

THE DOVE RETURNS

In the biblical story of the Flood, Noah released first a raven and then a dove to search for land. When the dove returned bearing an olive branch in its bill, this marked a new epoch after a time of loss and hardship, and so the bird came to stand as a symbol of peace and hope. The dove's universal associations with peace owe nothing to its nature – it is often quarrelsome – and much to its pure white beauty. Another important meaning attached to doves is the Holy Spirit: when John the Baptist baptized Christ he saw the Spirit of God descending upon him "like a dove". By meditating on the dove, we access the possibility of perceiving divinity in our hearts.

MYSTIC RINGS

LOVE, WHICH COMES FROM OUR UNADULTERATED SPIRIT, HAS THE CAPACITY TO BE

ETERNAL AND PURE. WE SPEAK OF "FOREVER" WITH NO THOUGHT OF MORTALITY,

BECAUSE MORTALITY SPEAKS A LANGUAGE FOREIGN TO THE PURE OF HEART.

THIS MANDALA FACILITATES A MYSTIC MARRIAGE WITH OUR BELOVED.

1 Focus on the pink shell in the centre of the mandala. Let its colour pour unconditional love into your heart. Let its spiral shape remind you that love is natural and beautiful.

2 Broaden your gaze out to the interlinked rings that form a *vesica piscis*, a sign of the sacred marriage of matter and spirit. Make a solemn promise to yourself that you will live in the spirit of this union.

3 Now follow the energy of love as its rays stream out from the Earth to honour the Sun and Moon. You have joined in a cosmic community of love. Remember the ending of Dante's *Il Paradiso*: "The love that moves the sun and other stars."

4 Finally, be enveloped in love's angelic wings as you glide effortlessly to the rim of the mandala. You are poised to fly free.

" ... the moments when you have truly lived are the moments when you have done things in the spirit of love. "

HENRY DRUMMOND (1851–1897)

LIKE A BUTTERFLY

17

IN HEALTHY RELATIONSHIPS, WE OFFER OTHERS HELP AND SUPPORT TO DEVELOP THEIR

POTENTIAL, ALLOWING THEM TO SPREAD THEIR WINGS AND BECOME MORE FULLY

THEMSELVES. THIS CAN TAKE COURAGE AND ENERGY, BUT TRANSFORMS BOTH GIVER

AND RECEIVER. USE THIS BUTTERFLY MANDALA TO SEE HOW MUCH YOU CAN GIVE.

1 Focus on the caterpillars and cocoons or chrysalises in the centre of the mandala. The butterfly growing inside each one expends its energy to break out and spread its wings. Relationships, too, need effort and energy.

2 Beyond, find the diamond-shaped space where a relationship can grow. Sense the adult butterflies' antennae alert to every movement. Alertness to another is a sign of love.

3 Next, shift your gaze to the four butterflies. They will take off in turn to find their destiny — first the upper two, then the two beneath, in an orderly dance of love.

4 Finally, focus on the suns and the moons in the circular rim of the mandala. A moon covers each sun, although without eclipsing it. The sun's rays blaze out undimmed. You feel at rest and in harmony.

Happiness is like a butterfly which, when pursued, is ... beyond our grasp, but if you will sit down quietly, may alight upon you.

NATHANIEL HAWTHORNE (1804–1864)

HEAVENLY HARMONY

"The Heavens themselves, the Planets, and this centre, observe degree, priority, and place."

WILLIAM SHAKESPEARE (1564—1616)

THE ILLUMINATED COSMOS

"The Word of God is the universal and invisible Light, cognizable by the senses, that emits its blaze in the Sun, Moon, Planets, and other Stars."

ALBERT PIKE (1809—1891)

A CELESTIAL PAIRING

The sun and moon exist on totally different scales of magnitude and distance – the moon is our diminuitive neighbour, the sun a fiery giant in another realm to whom we pay homage and from whom we receive protection. The difference between a sun and a satellite is vast. If in terms of symbolism they have a closer kinship, this is because our viewpoint sees them as heavenly bodies that rise and set, within the cycle of day and night. This near-sighted truth is valid, yet there is far-sighted wisdom beyond it: the sheer immensity of creation, the wonder of its unconquerable spaces, and the human spirit in the midst of it all – humble, eternal, proud and no less beautiful than sun or moon.

LADY OF COMPASSION

COMPASSION IS THE ROOT OF SPIRITUAL HEALING. IT IS PERSONALIZED HERE AS THE GODDESS OF COMPASSION, WHO DELAYED HER OWN SALVATION UNTIL SHE HAD SAVED ALL SOULS ON EARTH. SHE IS DEPICTED IN A MEDITATION POSE, SENDING HER LOVING-KINDNESS OUTWARD FROM A HEART FULL OF LOVE.

1 Focus on the Goddess of Compassion in the centre of the mandala. Open your heart to her unconditional love and acceptance. Feel confident that her endless compassion is pouring out to you, enabling you to be compassionate in turn.

2 Now rest in the ring of soft, heart-shaped petals. Feel the blooming of compassion inside yourself, like a warm glow.

3 Let your eyes drift to the little circles containing miniature deities. The Goddess of Compassion's tiny form can nestle inside every human heart, including yours. Think of these goddess in every atom of every in-breath and out-breath.

4 Take your gaze to the mandala's surround, the lovely flowers that bloom when compassion's seeds fall on fertile soil.

> *Our sorrows and wounds are healed only when we touch them with compassion.*
>
> **THE BUDDHA (C.563–C.483 BCE)**

THE MERCIFUL GODDESS

The Goddess of Compassion has been venerated in many cultures
under different guises – from Ancient Egypt's Isis to China's Kuan
Yin. In Tibet, she is known as Tara, the feminine aspect of the Buddha,
who as a *bodhisattva*, or enlightened being, chooses to forgo the
permanent bliss of Nirvana in order to help others. Her ancestor is the
male *bodhisattva*, Avalokiteshvara. She embodies unconditional love,
acceptance, mercy and forgiveness, and is often appealed to in times
of distress for protection, comfort and healing – she is known in all
cultures as "She who listens to the cries of the world". In one legend,
she is granted a thousand arms to help her in her endless almsgiving.

THE HEALING PATH

"If you want others to be happy, practise compassion.
If you want to be happy, practise compassion."

THE DALAI LAMA (BORN 1935)

COMPASSIONATE HEART

"Never let anyone come to you without coming away
better and happier."

ABBÉ GASTON COURTOIS (1897–1970)

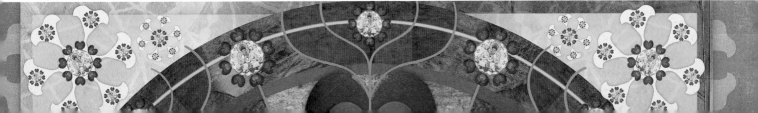

A CUP OVERFLOWING

THE CUP OF PLENTY IS A WISH-FULFILLING MAGIC VESSEL THAT FREELY BESTOWS

NOURISHMENT IN WHATEVER FORM IS REQUIRED. IN THIS MANDALA MEDITATION, IT

POURS FORGIVENESS — THE MOST EFFECTIVE BALM FOR HEALING THE HEART. BUT

YOU MAY ADAPT THE MEDITATION TO LOVE, OR PEACE, OR WISDOM IF YOU WISH.

1 Start by contemplating the spiral *bindu* at the very centre of the mandala — this is your self, saturated with the potential for forgiveness, and about to set off on the inner journey that will win it as your treasure.

2 Look at the centrally placed golden chalice, its water spilling abundantly onto the earth. Think of this as forgiveness in endless supply.

3 Meditate on the perfect pattern of reconciliation made by the flowing waters. Forgiveness forms around the pattern in your heart — a geometry of love and peace.

4 Travel out from the circle of potentiality — the round table on which the chalice stands. The first flowing circle is forgiveness in your heart. Move to the outer flowing circle — a commitment to *enacting* forgiveness.

> *In giving, a man receives more than he gives,*
> *and the more is in proportion to the worth of the thing given.*
>
> **GEORGE MACDONALD (1824–1905)**

KARMIC RECKONING

*"A human act once set in motion
flows on forever to the great account."*

GEORGE MEREDITH (1828–1909)

OUR HOLY GRAIL

*"For one human being to love another: that is perhaps
the most difficult of our tasks; the ultimate,
the last test and proof, the work for which
all other work is but preparation."*

RAINER MARIA RILKE (1875–1926)

THE CHALICE

In Irish legend, we encounter the chalice as the Cauldron of Dagda, which grants the wishes of all who come into its presence. Later, as the Holy Grail, a chalice becomes a central focus in the Arthurian legend, being available only to those who are worthy and who pass rigorous tests. In Christianity, the test is a call to faith: the Grail was thought to be the cup from which Christ drank at the Last Supper or in which blood was gathered from his side during the Crucifixion. To integrate the symbolic chalice into your own life, consider your soul as a vessel: valuable for what it contains, and carrying out its proper purpose only when full to the brim and beyond, not when sitting empty as a trophy.

ANOTHER'S FIRE

ONCE THE UNIQUE SPIRIT INSIDE YOU IS IGNITED BY A TRUE SENSE OF YOUR WORTH, IT BURNS AWAY THE DROSS TO ALLOW YOUR ESSENTIAL NATURE TO SHINE THROUGH. THIS MANDALA MOVES OUTSIDE THE SELF AND ASKS YOU TO INHABIT, SYMBOLICALLY, THE SPIRIT OF SOMEONE YOU KNOW — LOVED ONE, FRIEND, ACQUAINTANCE OR STRANGER.

1 Start with the pearl at the centre of the mandala — the spirit of your friend, in concentrated essence. All his or her thoughts, actions and emotions proceed from this pearl, fostered within the oyster of inheritance and experience.

2 See the flames of action radiate from this person as they move through life, connecting powerfully with those around them.

3 Observe how the blazing pearl of this person is at the centre of their own web of life. You yourself are a shining thread in this web — strong, connected and one of many.

4 Broaden your focus to take in the entire mandala — a beautiful outpouring of energy, constantly in motion yet always forming a perfect pattern around its centre. Send loving thoughts to feed your friend's flames.

> *The most powerful weapon on earth is the human soul on fire.*
>
> **FERDINAND FOCH (1851–1929)**

THE WEB OF LIFE

We are all part of a complex web of life. Every species on our planet, from the tiniest organism to the largest mammal, contributes to the health and balance of the whole. We might compare this to a spider's web, in which the slightest movement sends vibrations through the entire subtle yet resilient structure. Often, we feel the need for healing because we have lost our connection with other parts of this web — family, friends, a spiritual community. Begin to rediscover the energies of the web by strengthening bonds with loved ones. As you do so, watch how love and compassion fortify your inner life and spread out into the world, attracting kindred spirits to reconnect you to the whole.

MILLIONS TAKE PART

"In the entire universe there are myriad forms and millions of blades of grass, and each ... are, one by one, the entire universe."

DOGEN (1200–1253)

LINKS IN THE CHAIN OF BEING

"Earthworms, though in appearance a small and despicable link in the chain of nature, yet, if lost, would make a lamentable chasm."

GILBERT WHITE (1720–1793)

THE SELF IN TIMES OF CHALLENGE

Our bodies have an amazing capacity for regeneration
– broken bones knit together, damaged nerves re-grow,
mental and physical wounds heal over. We also, of course,
have immense reserves of patience and courage, if only we can
access them. Meditating on the ten mandalas in this chapter
helps you to find the strength and resourcefulness to overcome
illness, loss and loneliness so that, like the phoenix rising from
the ashes of its former self, you may even emerge from times
of difficulty rejuvenated in heart and mind.

SPIRAL RIVER

WATER TAKES THE PATH OF LEAST RESISTANCE, FLOWING WITH EASE AROUND

OBSTACLES AND ALWAYS MOVING ON. MEDITATING ON A RIVER, THEREFORE, HELPS

THE MIND TO STAY FLUID IN TROUBLED TIMES, INSTEAD OF FIGHTING THE CURRENT.

ALLOW THE RIVER'S ENERGY TO CARRY YOU TO NEW SHORES.

1 Rest your gaze on the central yin-yang symbol, sign of duality: the complementary opposites of life. Then follow the spiral flow of the water — a magic river without turbulence, which flows inside us all.

2 Take in the scenery as you float past the river banks: grasses give way to trees, which give way to rocks. All are unaffected by your problems, and so, in truth, are you.

3 Feel the persistent flow deepening the river by constant erosion of the river bed. Our resilience in the face of problems deepens us similarly: there is no difficulty life can throw at us that doesn't enable us to grow.

4 At the end of your spiral voyage, once you have weathered the immediate crisis, find yourself in a space of endless possibility. Your life is as rich as you choose.

"Water is fluid, soft and yielding. But water will wear away rock, which is rigid and cannot yield … what is soft is strong."

LAO TZU (C.604–C.531 BCE)

SPIRAL ENERGY

The spiral is a common shape in nature, found in the complex double-helix structure of DNA, in shells, coiled serpents, whirlpools and galaxies. When our distant ancestors began to make art, the shape was engraved into rocks and drawn on cave walls. This symbolic spiral is rich in meaning. It has come to represent evolution, the cycles of the seasons and of life, self-transformation, and the development of understanding, knowledge and wisdom. It also has links with feminine power and fertility (the inward spiral) and with masculine energy (the uncoiling spiral). The continuous concentric and progressive motion of the spiral suggests the very rhythm of life itself.

SPIRAL RHYTHMS

"Progress has not followed a straight ascending line, but a spiral with rhythms of progress and retrogression, of evolution and dissolution."

JOHANN WOLFGANG VON GOETHE (1749–1832)

A LIFE OF CHANGE

"Nothing is secure but life, transition, the energizing spirit."

RALPH WALDO EMERSON (1803–1882)

FLOATING CLOUDS

FEAR IS A NATURAL DEFENCE IN TIMES OF DANGER, BUT ALL TOO OFTEN OUR FEARS

ARE BASED, AT LEAST IN PART, ON IMAGINED PERILS. FAR BEYOND ITS CAUSE, FEAR

CAN GROW AND TAKE US OVER LIKE AN ALIEN LIFE-FORM. THIS MANDALA ENCOURAGES

YOU TO LET GO OF FEARS TO REVEAL YOUR TRUE, INDOMITABLE SELF.

1 Rest your gaze on the clouds within the mandala — fears that drift over the sky of consciousness. See how wispy they are: they fail to blot out the force of the sun — the strong centre of the mandala and of your being.

2 Now turn your attention to the sun as it sets over the still water. Feel its gentle warmth melting away the clouds moment by moment, and watch them losing even what strength they had. In the coming darkness, these clouds pose no threat.

3 Find the butterflies and birds on the rim of the mandala — the flight from fear is a journey toward wholeness.

4 Finally, bathe in the mandala as in a fortifying pool, breathing in its golden energy and its reflective peace.

> *The mind should be a vastness like the sky.*
> *Mental events should be allowed to disperse like clouds.*

LONGCHENPA (1308–1363)

TEARDROP HEALING

WHETHER YOU HAVE LOST A FRIEND, A LOVED ONE, A JOB OR A LONG-HELD DREAM,

GRIEVING IS A HEALING PROCESS THAT ENABLES US TO WORK THROUGH THE

PROGRESS OF NATURAL EMOTIONS TO ARRIVE IN THE END AT ACCEPTANCE AND

RESTORED PEACE. THIS MANDALA IS DESIGNED TO HELP THAT PROCESS.

1 Start at the dark centre of the mandala. Simply sit here with your feelings and halt the temptation to push grief away. Instead, give yourself space to simply feel.

2 Move your focus to the four streams of tears, recognizing their cooling, cleansing potential. See each tear as a healing drop of rain. Give yourself permission to let tears flow if you feel it will help.

3 Follow the tears, drop by drop, from the dark inner circle to the pale green outer circle — the zone of recovery. You may not feel ready to enter the outer zone wholeheartedly yet, but you will in time.

4 Gaze at the fresh growth springing from soil watered by tears — the shoots and full-blown flowers. These may represent wisdom now but later they may suggest renewal.

One's suffering disappears when one lets oneself go, when one yields — even to sadness.

ANTOINE DE SAINT-EXUPÉRY (1900–1944)

PURIFYING THE SOUL

"Wash away, Waters, whatever sin is in me, what wrong I have done, what imprecation I have uttered, and what untruth I have spoken."

RIG VEDA (C.1700–1000 BCE)

SORROW WILL PASS

"Soon the ice will melt, and the blackbirds sing along the river which he frequented, as pleasantly as ever."

HENRY DAVID THOREAU (1817–1862)

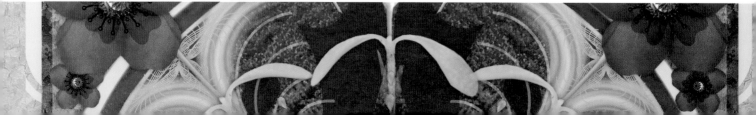

CLEANSING WATERS

Water cleanses. The purest waters are often thought to be dew and spring water – but also rain. Key characteristics are transparency (no deception, no cloudy emotions), and also the power to wash away stains and even obstructions. The sacred wells of the Celtic world intensify the mystic power of water and have the advantage, for the mandala meditator, of being circular, and therefore suggestive of eternity: you might visualize the mandala on page 130 as a well if you choose to. Other associations of water include fertility and fluidity. In troubled times, ask yourself which of water's qualities you need in order to get to the other side of the stormy sea unscathed.

REGENERATING SUN

WHEN, AT DIFFICULT TIMES, WE FEEL SEVERELY DEPLETED OF STRENGTH, WE CAN

DRAW ON THE NATURAL FORCES WITHIN, AROUND AND ABOVE US. IN THIS MANDALA,

THE FIRE OF THE SUN, THE LIGHT OF THE MOON AND THE STARS, AND THE RHYTHM

OF THE COSMOS ALL PROVIDE US WITH ALTERNATIVE SOURCES OF ENERGY.

1 Focus on the sunflower surrounded by a glowing sun, both symbols of vibrant life, inspiration and enthusiasm. Feel the fiery colours raise your spirits and your energy.

2 Take your attention to the four phases of the moon circling the sun, a reminder that all things have their phases and seasons. Be reassured that darkness makes way for light, and stale energy for fresh inspiration.

3 Shift your focus out to encompass the yin-yang symbol, which contains night and day. See the value in both aspects; observe how each rests within the other. Let the stars illuminate your darkness to show the path ahead. Let worries drift by like clouds.

4 Finally, view the whole mandala. Let the energy of the solar centre, and its surrounds, lift your spirits and feed your energy.

> *The art of healing comes from nature, not from the physician; because the physician must start from nature, with an open mind.*

PARACELSUS (1493–1541)

THE ALL-SEEING EYE

MANY CHALLENGES WE FACE REQUIRE US TO TAP INTO OUR DEEP INNER WELL OF
WISDOM — NOT LEAST FOR AN UNDERSTANDING OF HOW SERIOUS THE CHALLENGE
IS IN THE CONTEXT OF THE THINGS THAT REALLY MATTER. TAP INTO YOUR WISE SELF
AT THE CENTRE OF THIS MANDALA TO DEAL WITH DIFFICULT SITUATIONS.

1 Focus on the pupil at the centre of the mandala. Enter its darkness and move into the quiet space where your true wisdom lies.

2 Widen your gaze to take in the whole eye: your wise self looking back at you with confidence and calm.

3 Shift your attention out to the stylized eyes, taken from ancient Egyptian art. See these as keys to your deepest knowledge and skills, which you can call on at times of need. Visualize them opening doors of perception inside yourself.

4 Finally, bring the wise animals into focus. Let your innate wisdom tell you how to use the owl's ability to see from all angles and guide you in how to be strong and dignified, like the elephant.

We do not receive wisdom, we must discover it for ourselves, after a journey through the wilderness which no one else can make …

MARCEL PROUST (1871–1922)

SIGHT AND INSIGHT

The eye is a portal through which wisdom enters, whether from observation or from reading. Its pupil is a well, a mandala, an unfathomable depth. Traditionally, symbols of sight range from the Eye of Horus (denoting the wisdom of the falcon sky god in ancient Egypt) to the Eye of Vishnu in India, whose every blink is thought to mark the passing of an epoch. Eyes, the windows of the soul, may be accompanied by a psychic "third eye" at the forehead, associated with intuition and wise perception. The eye is linked with the "I" that observes the world. In meditation, you encourage this "I" to look inside, trawling your deepest inner realms for the keys to self-knowledge.

WAYS OF SEEING

"How can the divine Oneness be seen? … If you are willing to be lived by it, you will see it everywhere, even in the most ordinary things."

LAO TZU (C.604–C.531 BCE)

A FLASH OF LIGHT

"Intuition is the clear conception of the whole at once."

JOHANN KASPAR LAVATER (1741–1801)

PHOENIX RISING

THE HUMAN BODY HAS AMAZING POWERS OF SELF-HEALING (JUST THINK OF A CUT IN THE SKIN) AND REGENERATION. FINDING CALM IN MEDITATION CAN HELP US TO DEAL EVEN WITH SERIOUS ILLNESSES, AS WELL AS WITH STRESS, LISTLESSNESS AND DEPRESSION. PHOENIX-LIKE (SEE PAGE 142), WE CAN RISE ANEW FROM DAMAGE.

1 Contemplate the rising phoenix, symbol of your invincible spirit. Imagine it giving you its blessing, the feathery tips of its wings stroking your body with slow, healing magic.

2 Focus on the apple, an emblem of your trust in nature, and the clusters of fruit that represent your practical plan for well-being (make one in advance, perhaps including good diet and exercise).

3 Now find the white dove that represents all that inspires you — faith in nature, hope for the future, belief in the spirit.

4 Finally, meditate on the triangle with a spot at its centre — the emblem of elemental fire. This is where your fears and your sickness burn away, and you can find liberation. Shed your anxieties as you meditate on the core of your invulnerable true self.

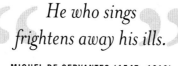

He who sings frightens away his ills.

MIGUEL DE CERVANTES (1547–1616)

THE FIREBIRD

The phoenix symbolizes regeneration. According to a legend that arose in Heliopolis, ancient centre of Egyptian sun worship, the phoenix was a male bird of great longevity – living for 500 years or more. Only one of these beautiful creatures could live at any one time. When its end drew near, the phoenix faced the rising sun in the east, built itself a nest of aromatic twigs and sang so enchantingly that even the sun god paused on his journey. As a spark from the sun ignited its nest, the phoenix died in the flames and was born anew. It then flew to the sun god with its ashes as an offering. The phoenix has been associated with Christ's resurrection and with the awakening faith of spiritual initiates.

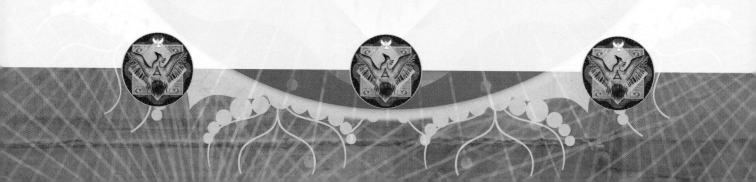

....

PRECIOUS FUEL

"The fire that burns is the fire that gives life, and sometimes the best fuel is something precious to us."

GIUSEPPE MARASPINI (1845–1910)

THE PROMISE OF RENEWAL

"As the same person inhabits the body through childhood, youth and old age, so too at the time of death he attains another body."

***BHAGAVAD GITA* (1ST OR 2ND CENTURY BCE)**

DRAGON POWER

A DRAGON REPRESENTS THE PASSIONATE ENERGY WITHIN YOU, OFFERING PROTECTION

FROM DANGER AND STANDING GUARD OVER THE HIDDEN TREASURE OF YOUR INNER

NATURE. WHEN YOU FEEL THREATENED OR FEARFUL, USE THIS MANDALA TO CALL

UPON YOUR INNER GUARDIAN TO GIVE YOU COURAGE AND KEEP YOU SAFE.

1 Meditate on the spiral at the centre of the mandala, symbolizing your life energy. Notice that it lies within the protective shell of an egg. Feel this shell nurturing and cradling your bottomless reserves of energy.

2 Now tap into the power of the dragon, which makes you and protects you. This is the strength that you summon from your energy reserves when you are under pressure.

3 The dragon is in a ring, with its tail to its mouth — emblem of the indivisible spirit. This provides all the energy you need to be yourself and protect yourself — if you have enough energy, these are the same thing.

4 Beyond the diamond of protective flames, gaze at the open clam shells with pearls on them — dragon power makes you feel safe enough to open up to others.

> *For an impenetrable shield,*
> *stand inside yourself.*
>
> **HENRY DAVID THOREAU (1817–1862)**

WORLD WITHOUT END

"I am Alpha and Omega, the beginning and the ending ... which is, and which was, and which is to come ..."

REVELATION (1:8)

ENDLESS RENEWAL

"Still ending, and beginning still."

WILLIAM COWPER (1731–1800)

THE CIRCLE OF RENEWAL

The ouruboros is a snake or dragon that swallows its tail to form the shape of a circle. The creature is integral to many creation myths, where it is described as encircling the world, holding our globe in a protective embrace. It symbolizes primordial unity, self-sufficiency and the cycles of nature – most obviously the regenerating force of creation that emerges out of destruction. The ouroboros represents an unfolding process of renewal: the alpha and omega, the beginning and the end. All that is known and unknown is contained within its ambit, and in some images the egg that it holds between its claws symbolizes the Philosopher's Stone, the fount of all knowledge.

GOLDEN CROSS

IT IS SAID THAT FEW OF US KNOW OUR OWN STRENGTH. WE MOST OFTEN FIND IT WHEN

WE LEAST EXPECT IT, IN TESTING TIMES. IN THIS MANDALA — ANOTHER THAT HELPS US

TO ACCESS INNER RESOURCES — WE DRAW POWER FROM THE UNIVERSAL SYMBOL OF

THE CROSS, OVERLAID WITH THE ROSE, IN A COMPOSITE EMBLEM OF POTENT HEALING.

1 Focus on the rose in the centre of the mandala. Recognize its beauty. This is your inner strength — delicate yet powerful. Let the potency of your inner rose unfold.

2 Now gaze at the cross, where matter and spirit meet. Your greatest strength comes as you access the point of connection. Visualize yourself centred and solid, strengthened by indestructible spirit.

3 Now shift your attention to the rays that burst out from the cross. They represent your inner starlight, a unique destiny that illuminates your life — a refulgence that gives your time on Earth glorious meaning.

4 Finally, look at the small roses on the circular perimeter. Strength needs only to be felt, not displayed: you can show the gentler side of yourself instead, even in hard times.

> *"A man's true state of power and riches is to be in himself."*
>
> **HENRY WARD BEECHER (1813–1887)**

A UNIVERSAL SYMBOL

One of our most ancient and universal symbols, the cross resonates
with profoud meanings, making it rich as an object of meditation.
Principally, it denotes the intersection of earthly life and spirit – and in
this respect may be seen as a simplification of The Tree of Life. A cross
can also represent the four directions and the four seasons – the energy
of nature's life-force. The ancient Egyptian *ankh* (a cross with a loop
at the top instead of the upper arm) and the Celtic cross encompassed
by a circle both have associations with eternal life – celebrating (in an
obvious link with the Christian cross) the triumph over death
and suffering, and the enduring nature of the spirit.

SPIRITUAL ORIENTATION

*"As a needle turns to the north, so I turn to the spirit
and all my fleshly being knows where truth lies."*

JULIANA PEREIRA (1895–1976)

THE CRUX OF NOW

*"Embrace the cross of the present, the eternal now
where illusions perish in a bountiful fire."*

KOSTAS LASKARI (1910–2001)

THE JAWS OF THE LION

IN THE ROYAL LION HUNT OF ANTIQUITY, COMMON IN WESTERN ASIA, THE KILLING OF THE GOD-LIKE SOLAR LION GUARANTEED THE CONTINUATION OF LIFE. WE SOMETIMES NEED TO SUPPRESS WHAT IS MOST OBVIOUSLY POWERFUL IN OURSELVES TO REACH A DEEPER SOURCE OF STRENGTH IN DIFFICULT TIMES.

1 Be brave and look into the mouth of the lion. This is the Other, yet also something found in ourselves — our animal nature, from which our instincts stem (as distinct from our intuitions, which are more refined).

2 Now let your gaze rest on the lion's teeth. You have your weapons if you choose to use them. Yet you also have love, wisdom and faith, which are likely to be more effective.

3 Look at the lion's head. A lion can roar loudly but the wisdom of our inner silence is likely to serve us better than a show of aggression or an attention-seeking cry.

4 Finally, take your attention to the battlements around the lion's head: they will keep the fortress of your soul safe from harm. You have as much presence in the world as the mighty lion, and a nobler destiny.

> *Bravery is stability, not of legs and arms,*
> *but of courage and the soul.*

MICHEL DE MONTAIGNE (1533–1592)

LOTUS HARVEST

THE LOTUS STANDS FOR PURITY AND ENLIGHTENMENT, THE ABILITY OF THE SELF TO GROW OUT OF FLESHY ORIGINS — THE MUD AT THE BOTTOM OF THE LAKE — AND BLOOM WITH SPIRITUAL BEAUTY. THE MUD MAY EVOKE TRANSIENCE, THE INEVITABILITY THAT YOUTH WILL FADE; BUT WISDOM COUNSELS US TO ACCEPT AND REJOICE.

1 Focus on the lotus at the centre of the mandala. It has opened to beauty, despite its humble origins in mud; and this beauty comes from the very core of the self.

2 Shift your focus to the blue of the lake water shimmering with reflections. This is a place to bathe and find calm, confident in the knowledge of your spiritual maturity. Feel the cool waters refreshing you.

3 Gaze at the six lotus blossoms around the central flower. Let the seven blooms drift in your consciousness as you relax in pleasant thoughts. Time passes but the moment gives ample space for contentment.

4 Finally, look at the corn stalks in the corners of the square, symbolizing the growing self. Sink into the peace that comes with this knowledge of your spiritual harvest.

> *The harvest treasures all*
> *Now gathered in, beyond the range of storms.*
>
> **JAMES THOMSON (1700–1748)**

NATURE AND SPIRIT

When applied to the mind and spirit, as distinct from the body, healing is more than a metaphor, because our bodies are not the only part of us that can suffer ill health – our inner self can too, and so can our relationships with others, with the cosmos and with the One. Nature provides an organic pharmacy that equips us to heal these intangible rifts and imbalances. Just as herbs can fix our bodily ills, the imagery of nature, taken internally, can work on our mental and spiritual issues and promote gentle repair. This is as unobtrusive as healing gets: we just take into conciousness a floral mandala, or a real flower, and allow ourselves to be worked on by the best medicine in the cosmos.

PURE DEPTHS

*"Simply always let go
and make your heart empty and open.
Be like the stillness of water,
like the clarity of a mirror."*

TA HUI (1088—1163)

ROOT AND BLOOM

"My mind is a flower, meditation my roots."

AHMET NEDIM (1681—1730)

FURTHER READING

Bell, B. and Todd, D. *GaiaStar Mandalas: Ecstatic Visions of the Living Earth* Pomegranate Communications, Petaluna (USA), 2002

Brennan B., Smith A. *Hands of Light: A Guide to Healing Through the Human Energy Field* Bantam Books Ltd, New York, 1990

Chaitow, L. *Conquer Pain the Natural Way* Duncan Baird Publishers, London, 2007

Brownstein, A. *Extraordinary Healing: The Amazing Power of Your Body's Secret Healing System* Harbor Press Inc., Gig Harbor (USA), 2005

Cole, J. *Ceremonies of the Seasons* Duncan Baird Publishers, London and New York, 2007

Cornell, J. *Mandala: Luminous Symbols for Healing* Quest Books, Wheaton (USA), 2006

Cornell, J. *The Mandala Healing Kit* Sounds True Audio, Louisville (USA), 2006

Cunningham, B. *Mandala: Journey to the Centre* Dorling Kindersley Publishing, New York, 2003

Dahlke, R. *Mandalas of the World: A Meditating and Painting Guide* Sterling Publishing Company Inc., 2005

Dahlke, R. *Mandalas for Meditation* Sterling Publishing Company Inc., New York, 2002

Mind, Body and Spirit Companion: Exercises and Meditations to Free Your Spirit and Fulfil Your Dreams Duncan Baird Publishers, London, and One Spirit, New York, 2006

Emoto M. *The True Power of Water: Healing and Discovering Ourselves* Atria Books, New York, 2005

Fontana, D. *The Secret Language of Symbols* Duncan Baird Publishers, London, and Chronicle Books, San Francisco, 2003

Fontana, D. *Meditating with Mandalas* Duncan Baird Publishers, London, 2005

Fontana, D. *Learn to Meditate* Duncan Baird Publishers, London, and Chronicle Books, San Francisco, 1999

Hay, L. *You Can Heal Your Life* Hay House Inc., Carlsbad (USA), 2002

Hinz, Drs M. & J. *Learn to Balance Your Life* Duncan Baird Publishers, London, 2004

Huyser, A. *Mandala Workbook for Inner Self-Development* Binkey Kok Publications, Haarlem (NL), 2002

Levine, P. *Waking the Tiger: Healing Trauma – The Innate Capacity to Transform Overwhelming Experiences* North Atlantic Books, Berkeley (USA), 1997

McLeod, J. *Colours of the Soul: Transform Your Life Through Colour Therapy* O Books, Berkeley (USA), 2006

Parlett, S. *Crystal Meditation Kit* Duncan Baird Publishers, London, and Barnes and Noble, New York, 2005

Rose, E. M. & Dalto, A. R. *Create Your Own Sand Mandala Kit* Red Wheel Weiser, Newburyport (USA), 2004

Selby, A. *The Chakra Energy Plan* Duncan Baird Publishers, London and New York, 2006

Tenzin-Dolma, L. *Natural Mandalas* Duncan Baird Publishers, London and New York, 2006

Tucci, G. *The Theory and Practice of the Mandala* Dover Publications, Mineola (USA), 2001

Virtue, D. *Chakra Clearing: Awakening Your Spiritual Power to Know and Heal* (Book and CD) Hay House Inc., Carlsbad (USA), 2003

GENERAL INDEX

For ease of reference, this index has been divided into two parts: the first is an index of concepts that occur throughout the book; the second is an index of specific symbols.

A
acupuncture 11
architectural structures 35, 96, 153
auras 30–31

B
balance 10, 11, 69, 89
bindu 20, 22, 38
brainwaves 21
Buddhism 35, 44, 45, 46, 112, 157

C
Celtic symbols 38, 133, 150
chakras 30, 31, 69, 89, 91
change 17, 55, 70, 72–3, 82–3
Chinese traditions 17, 19, 72, 112
Christianity 46, 117, 150
colours 32–3, 90, 91, 104, 154
compassion 110, 112–13, 120
consciousness 22, 38
courage 77, 153
creativity 61

D
directions 43, 150, 151
Dogon traditions 19

dreams 25
Dreamtime 19

E
Egyptian symbols 112, 138, 150
elements 43, 70
energy 11, 28, 30–31, 81, 134, 145
enlightenment 17, 154

F
fear 128, 153

G
geometric shapes 36, 38, 40, 56
Greek myths 46, 77
grief 131, 132–3

H
harmony 16, 26, 46, 48, 89, 95, 107, 108–9
healing 9–10, 134
  focus 25–7, 28–9
  symbols 25, 34–5
healing energy practice 27
healing, vibrational 11, 32
Holy Grail 117
homeopathy 11
hope and renewal 56, 101, 140, 142–3, 145–7

I
I Ching 70, 72
impermanence 17, 41, 46, 58
Indian traditions 17, 19, 138
individuation 24
infinity 36
intuition 12, 25, 29, 64, 89, 137, 139
Isis 112

J
Jung, Carl 5, 16, 20, 24

K
Kalachakra 17
Kuan Yin 44, 112

L
love 56, 75, 77, 101, 104, 110, 112–13, 115–16, 120

M
mandalas
  benefits 9, 10
  choosing 31, 35, 49
  definition 9, 13, 28
  how to use 14, 48–51
  hypnotic effect 21
  key elements 22
  in the landscape 17–19

as maps of well-being 20–22
  through the ages 17
Mary (Virgin) 46
medicine wheels 19
meditation
  benefits 10, 12, 156
  and mandalas 9, 10, 11, 12, 13–14, 16, 48–51
  and mantras 12
mind, body, spirit 84
motion 70

N
Native American traditions 19
nature 36, 40–42
Noah 103
number symbolism 39

O
One, The 38, 48, 98, 156

P
peace 101–103, 154
Philosopher's Stone 147
purity 56, 75, 77, 154

R
reiki 11
relationships 95, 101, 107
relaxation 10, 13, 154

Roman myths 46, 77

S
sacred wells 133
sand mandalas 19, 46
seasons 43, 45, 58, 134
self 24, 56, 61, 84, 92, 96
sight and insight 137–9
soul 55, 59, 63, 76, 77, 84, 118, 138
spirit 43, 84, 154
strength 69, 77, 148, 153
symbolism 16, 17, 25, 34–45

T
Tibetan traditions 17, 22, 45–6, 112
truth 56, 99

U
unconscious mind 22, 24–5
universe 16, 27, 44, 55, 61, 121

W
wisdom 75, 96, 137, 138

INDEX OF SYMBOLS

A
acorns 69
air 43, 70, 95
animals 42, 137
apples 140

B
baby 55
beads 84
birds 42, 61, 63, 92, 96, 115, 128
Bodhisattvas 44, 112
butterflies 107, 128

C
caterpillars 107
chains 81
chakras 69, 89, 91
chalices 89, 115, 117
chrysanthemums 56
circles 22, 36–8, 78, 110, 147
clouds 43, 67, 128, 134
cocoons 107
corn 154
cosmos 19, 44–5, 55, 56, 96
cranes 42, 95
crosses 35, 92, 148, 150
cup of plenty 115
cycles of nature 131, 147

D
daffodils 56
diamonds 75, 76, 77
DNA 55, 126
domes 35, 96
doves 101–103, 140
dragons 42, 145, 147

E
eagles 42, 62
earth 43, 70, 95
eggs 55, 145, 147
elephants 137
eyes 96, 137, 138

F
fire 43, 70, 118, 140
fish 64
flames 43, 61, 118, 145
flowers 41, 56, 58–9, 92, 101, 110, 115, 131
flying 61, 62–3, 101, 104
fruit 140

G
globe 14, 27, 104, 147
Goddess of Compassion 44, 110, 112–13

H
hands 92
Healing Buddha 44

hexagrams 72
horses 81
human figures 45–6, 55, 56, 64, 69
humming birds 92

J
jewels 75

L
laurel leaves 81
leaves 78, 81, 83, 95, 125
lemniscates 89
light 67, 70, 95, 108
lily pads 78
lions 42, 153
lotus 41, 75, 154

M
marriage 104
masculine and feminine 89, 126
mirrors 92
moon 45, 64, 66–7, 104, 107, 109, 134
mountains 43

O
oak trees 41, 69
olive branches 101, 102–3
OM 61

ouroboros 147
owls 42, 137

P
pearls 75, 145
pentacles 56
peonies 56
phoenix 42, 140, 142–3
planets 19, 44–5, 108

R
rainbows 89, 90–91
raindrops 9, 91
rings 104
rivers 64, 125
rocks 43, 64, 125
roses 35, 41, 56, 148

S
shells 36, 84, 104, 126, 145
sky 43
snowdrops 56, 58
space 43, 55, 107
spirals 19, 36, 36, 55, 70, 84, 104, 125, 126–7, 145
squares 22, 38, 81
Star of David 61
stars 40, 56, 64, 70, 77, 96, 134, 148
stupas 35

sun 45, 75, 104, 107–9, 128, 134, 142
sunflowers 78, 134
swords 89

T
Tara 44, 45–6, 112
tears 77, 131
temples 35, 96
Tree of Life 38, 150
trees 40–41, 69, 95
triangles 38, 61, 140
trigrams 70, 72
trinity 38, 84

V
vesica piscis 104

W
water 9, 43, 70, 75, 78, 115, 125, 128, 131–133, 154, 157
web of life 118, 120–121
wheel of the year 70
willows 41, 78
winds 81, 82–3
wings 101, 104, 107, 140

Y
yin-yang 46, 48, 72, 92, 95, 125, 134

ACKNOWLEDGMENTS

The publisher would like to thank the following people, museums, and photographic libraries for permission to reproduce their material. Every care has been taken to trace copyright holders. However, if we have omitted anyone we apologize and will, if informed, make corrections to any future edition.
PICTURE CREDITS: Page 8 Corbis/Zefa/ Matthias Kulka; **15** NASA; **18** Corbis/George H.H. Huey; **23** Corbis/Alen MacWeeney; **37** Getty Images/National Geographic/Darlyne

A. Murawski; **47** Corbis/Jeremy Horner.
TEXT CREDITS: Page 5 From *Memories, Dreams and Reflections* by C.G. Jung, edited by Aniela Jaffe, translated by Richard and Clara Winston, copyright © 1961, 1962, 1963 and renewed 1989, 1990, 1991. Used by permission of Pantheon Books, a division of Random House, Inc. **Page 61** Reprinted by permission of the publishers and the Trustees of Amherst College from *The Poems of Emily Dickinson: Reading Edition*, edited by Ralph W. Franklin,

F1686. Cambridge, Mass.: The Belknap Press of Harvard University Press, copyright © 1998, 1999 by the President and Fellows of Harvard College. Copyright © 1951, 1955, 1979, 1983 by the President and Fellows of Harvard College. **Page 113** From *Path to Enlightenment* by the Dalai Lama, copyright © 1997 by Kyabje Tenzin Gyatso, permission of the Wylie Agency. **Page 131** From *Southern Mail* by Antoine de Saint-Exupéry © copyright Éditions Gallimards.